100 Indians who made history

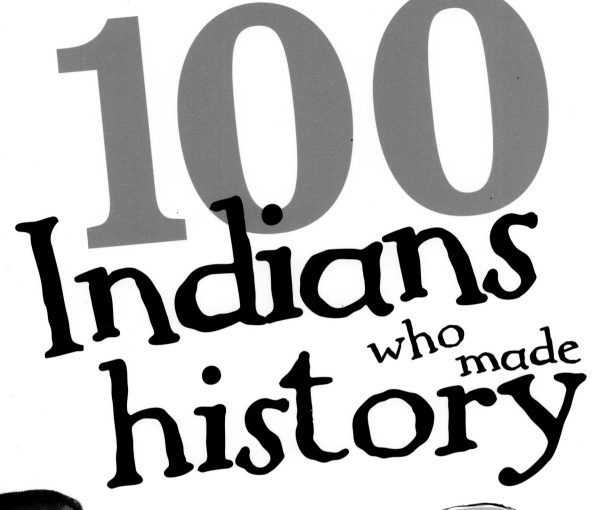

Meet the people who shaped modern India

**London, New York,
Melbourne, Munich, and Delhi**

Editorial team Medha Gupta, Suparna Sengupta, Dipali Singh
Design team Shrabani Dasgupta, Astha Singh, Sukriti Sobti
Illustrators Shrabani Dasgupta, Arun Pottirayil, Astha Singh, Sukriti Sobti

Picture researcher Sumedha Chopra
Picture research manager Taiyaba Khatoon

Managing editor Alka Ranjan
Design consultant Shefali Upadhyay

DTP designers Nandkishor Acharya,
Ganesh Sharma, Sachin Singh
Production manager Pankaj Sharma
Jacket designers Astha Singh, Sukriti Sobti

Vice president production Subhasis Ganguli
Managing director Aparna Sharma

First published in India in 2014
by Dorling Kindersley Publishing Private Ltd,
8, Local Shopping Centre, Panchsheel Park,
New Delhi 110017, India

2 4 6 8 10 9 7 5 3 1
257059 – 08/14

A CIP catalogue for this book is available from the British Library.

ISBN: 978-1-4093-4824-5

Dorling Kindersley India has made every effort to obtain information for
100 Indians who made history from credible sources. The book, however, does not
constitute an authorized biography of any of the personalities included in it.

Printed and bound in New Delhi
by Thomson Press India Ltd.

Discover more at
www.dk.com

100 Indians
who made
history

Meet the people who shaped modern India

Contents

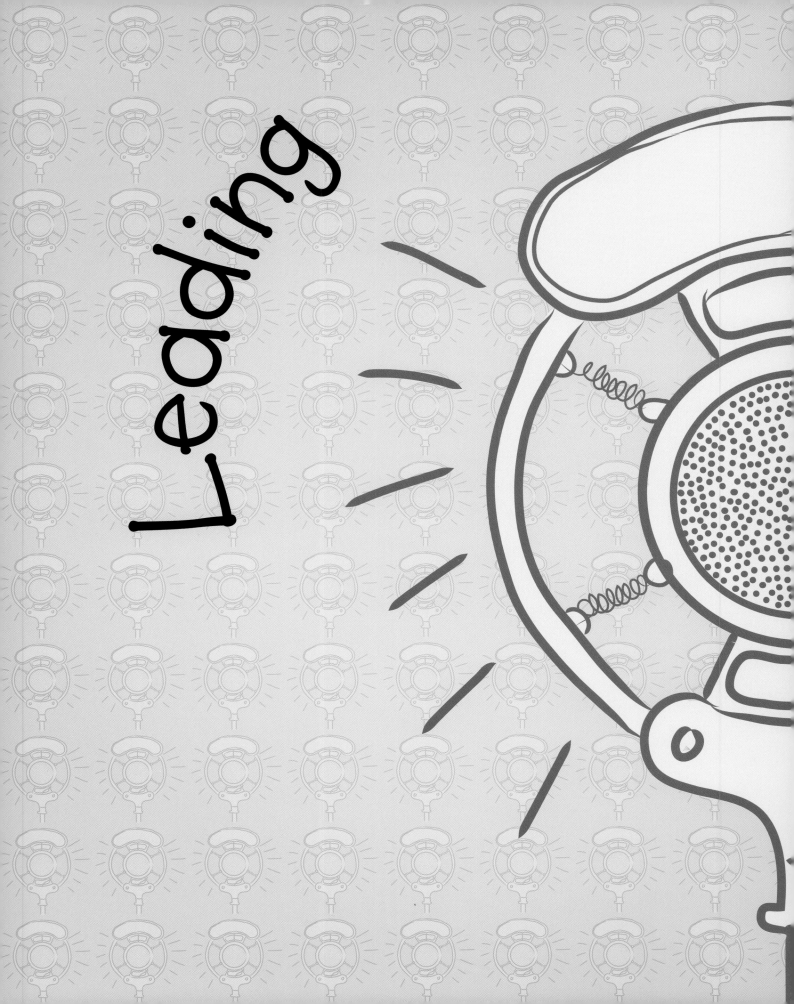

Leaders

These Indians made their mark by showing the way forward. Some had a thirst for battle, power, and glory, and won great empires and riches. Others kicked out their rulers because they thought they could do a better job. But they didn't all want to start a fight; a few just wanted peace and equality. Whether kings or queens or freedom fighters, these leaders were very good at telling other people what to do.

Chanakya & Chandragupta Maurya

The men who created the great MAURYAN EMPIRE

This adviser–king duo built an empire so vast that it brought most of India under one rule for the first time in history.

By the way... I would add small amounts of poison to Chandragupta's meals every day to make him immune to venom and protect him from enemies who tried to poison him.

When Chanakya met Chandragupta

In 326BCE, Alexander the Great, the Greek Emperor, reached India after conquering most of Asia. Legend has it that when he posed a threat to the city of Taxila, in northwest India, the people of Taxila turned to Chanakya (c. 350–275BCE), a respected teacher at Taxila University. Chanakya went to Pataliputra (now Patna), capital of Magadha, for help. However, **he was insulted and thrown out by the Nanda King**. On his way back to Taxila, he met a young boy called Chandragupta Maurya (340–298BCE). Chanakya took the boy with him and *the two started plotting revenge against the Nanda king*.

The making of a king

When Alexander died in 323BCE, Chanakya and Chandragupta seized the opportunity to **take control of Taxila and other areas in northwest India with the help of a small army they had put together**. They later moved towards Pataliputra and around 321BCE defeated the Nanda King of Magadha and **ESTABLISHED THE MAURYAN EMPIRE**.

They couldn't have done it without...

Written more than 2,300 years ago, **ARTHASHASTRA** *is Chanakya's detailed work on* **POLITICS, ECONOMY, AND HOW TO GOVERN.** *This book became a guide for Chanakya and Chandragupta to govern the newly established Mauryan Empire.*

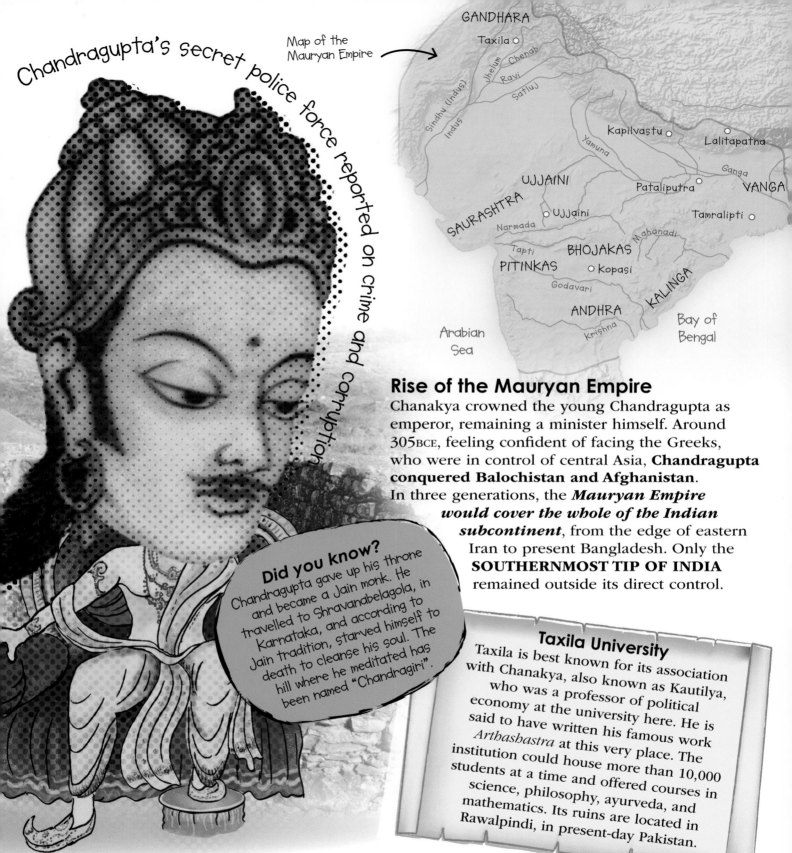

Chandragupta's secret police force reported on crime and corruption

Map of the Mauryan Empire →

GANDHARA
Taxila
Chenab
Jhelum
Ravi
Sindhu (Indus)
Satluj
Indus
Kapilvastu
Lalitapatha
Yamuna
Ganga
UJJAINI
Pataliputra
VANGA
SAURASHTRA
Ujjaini
Narmada
Tamralipti
Tapti
BHOJAKAS
Mahanadi
PITINKAS
Kopasi
KALINGA
Godavari
ANDHRA
Arabian
Sea
Krishna
Bay of
Bengal

Rise of the Mauryan Empire

Chanakya crowned the young Chandragupta as emperor, remaining a minister himself. Around 305BCE, feeling confident of facing the Greeks, who were in control of central Asia, **Chandragupta conquered Balochistan and Afghanistan.** In three generations, the *Mauryan Empire would cover the whole of the Indian subcontinent*, from the edge of eastern Iran to present Bangladesh. Only the **SOUTHERNMOST TIP OF INDIA** remained outside its direct control.

Did you know?
Chandragupta gave up his throne and became a Jain monk. He travelled to Shravanabelagola, in Karnataka, and according to Jain tradition, starved himself to death to cleanse his soul. The hill where he meditated has been named "Chandragiri".

Taxila University

Taxila is best known for its association with Chanakya, also known as Kautilya, who was a professor of political economy at the university here. He is said to have written his famous work *Arthashastra* at this very place. The institution could house more than 10,000 students at a time and offered courses in science, philosophy, ayurveda, and mathematics. Its ruins are located in Rawalpindi, in present-day Pakistan.

They paved the way for...

Chandragupta's grandson, **ASHOKA THE GREAT** *(ruled 273–232BCE) further extended the Mauryan Empire. He later turned against war after conquering* **KALINGA**, *in present-day Odisha.*

Ashoka the Great

The fierce warrior who later turned into a COMPASSIONATE EMPEROR

One of the most powerful emperors of India, Ashoka's life was a journey from a power-hungry, merciless ruler to a believer in "ahimsa", or "non-violence".

Accession to the throne

Ashoka (304–232BCE) was born to Mauryan Emperor Bindusara and Maharani Dharma. **His grandfather, Chandragupta Maurya**, was the founder of the Mauryan Empire. Right from his childhood days, *Ashoka showed great skill in handling weapons* and had a keen interest in warfare. Ashoka had many brothers who wanted to take the throne after their father's death, but he fought and killed all of them to **BECOME THE KING OF MAGADHA**, in present-day Bihar. After becoming the King, Ashoka **fought many wars to expand his empire**. He was a *ruthless ruler*, ready to do anything to conquer.

By the way... my grandfather Chandragupta Maurya threw away his sword when he left his empire to live a non-violent life. Just a boy at the time, I found the sword and kept it.

The war machine

Ashoka's **reign of terror continued for eight years**, earning him the name "Chandashok", or "Terrible Ashoka". At the peak of his kingship, his empire stretched from the Hindu Kush Mountains in Afghanistan in the northwest to present-day Bangladesh and Assam in the east, and to parts of Tamil Nadu and Andhra Pradesh in the south. He fought his last battle at **KALINGA, IN PRESENT-DAY ODISHA**, which proved to be a turning point in his life. This fierce battle made **him realize the bad consequences of war.**

This sculpture, found in the Queen's Cave of Udaygiri, Bhubaneswar, shows the Kalinga War.

The Sanchi Stupa built by Emperor Ashoka is one of the oldest stone structures in India. The Stupa contains the relics of the Buddha.

Pillars of Ashoka

Ashoka **erected pillars throughout the Magadha Empire to spread Gautam Buddha's messages**. These pillars, called "**ASHOKA STAMBH**", have the teachings of Buddhism and Ashoka's philosophies inscribed on them. At the top of each pillar is the sculpture of an animal (usually a lion or bull) and an inverted lotus flower. The most famous is the Ashoka pillar located at **Sarnath**, near Varanasi, which is believed to be the *site where Lord Buddha preached his first sermon*. The lion sculpture on top of the Sarnath pillar was later adopted as the **NATIONAL EMBLEM** of India.

When fierceness turned to faith

More than 100,000 people had lost their lives in the Kalinga War. Saddened by the sufferings of the defeated people, **Ashoka vowed to give up war** and adopt the path of peace shown by Gautam Buddha. He *made Buddhism his state religion* and helped spread its messages around the world, sending envoys as far as ancient Rome and Egypt. He sent his son, Mahindra, and daughter, Sanghamitra, to Ceylon (now Sri Lanka) to spread Buddhist ideas.

This Ashoka Stambh, or Ashokan Pillar, located within the Qutub Minar complex in Delhi, is made of iron that has not rusted over centuries.

The wheel of law

The 24-spoke wheel at the centre of our national flag is called the "Ashoka Chakra". Each spoke represents a principle of Buddhism. It is named after Ashoka as it appears on many Ashokan pillars.

He couldn't have done it without...

CHANDRAGUPTA MAURYA *(340–298BCE) was Ashoka's grandfather and the founder of the Mauryan Empire. Ashoka later inherited the throne from his father, Bindusara, and expanded the empire further.*

GAUTAM BUDDHA'S *(563–483BCE) teachings form the basis of Buddhism. Inspired by his philosophy, Ashoka transformed himself from a cruel warrior to a messenger of peace.*

All about me

- **BORN:** 1542
- **DIED:** 1605
- **PLACE OF BIRTH:** Umerkot, Pakistan
- **FACTOID:** I shifted my capital from Agra to Fatehpur Sikri, a popular tourist destination now.
- **IN A NUTSHELL:** I borrowed the best ideas from different religions and came up with a new religion, *Din-i-Ilahi*, or Divine Faith.

Akbar invited people from different faiths to his court.

Ahead of his time

Akbar was **only 13 years old when he ascended the Mughal throne** in 1556 after the death of his father, Humayun. Bairam Khan, Humayun's close associate, mentored the young emperor as his regent. A great conqueror, Akbar expanded his empire in successful military campaigns to include most of the Indian subcontinent. During his reign, *people from all religious backgrounds enjoyed equal treatment*. He showed interest in the religious and social customs of different people, and floated the idea of *Sulh-i-kul*, or "Universal Peace". He introduced a **SYSTEM OF TAXATION** that was fair to all.

Akbar
The GREATEST Mughal Emperor

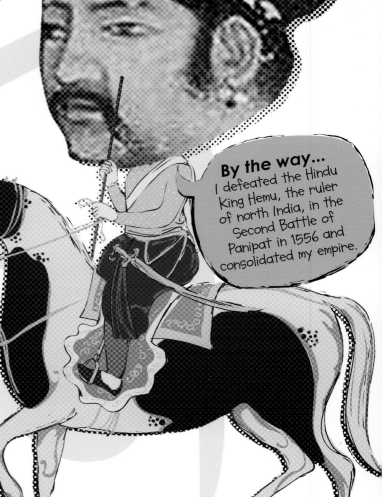

By the way...
I defeated the Hindu King Hemu, the ruler of north India, in the Second Battle of Panipat in 1556 and consolidated my empire.

Akbar's nine gems

Akbar could not read or write, yet he was a great patron of art and culture and invited the best minds to his court. **Nine such extraordinary talents were known as Akbar's nine gems**. Among these were Abul Fazl, the author of **Akbarnama** – the book that recounts Akbar's life in great detail; **MIAN TANSEN**, a Hindustani classical singer of unparalleled fame; and Birbal, Akbar's advisor who was known for his ready wit and wisdom.

All about me

- **BORN:** 1592
- **DIED:** 1666
- **PLACE OF BIRTH:** Lahore, Pakistan
- **FACTOID:** I hired 22,000 labourers from different parts of the world, who took 22 years to build the Taj Mahal.
- **IN A NUTSHELL:** I became the fifth Mughal Emperor, inheriting the throne after the death of my father, Jehangir.

Shah Jehan

The Mughal Emperor who gave the world the TAJ MAHAL

King of the world

Emperor Akbar named his grandson Khurram, meaning "**joyful**" **in Persian**. Ambitious from the very beginning, Prince Khurram led successful military campaigns in the Deccan, as well as against the Mewar kingdom in the west and the princely states of Kashmir in the north. So impressed was Emperor Jehangir with his military prowess that he gave him the title **SHAH JEHAN**, or "*Emperor of the world*".

By the way... my Peacock Throne, later stolen from India, was made of 1,150kg (2,535lb) of gold and 230kg (507lb) of precious stones. It is valued at more than 450 crore rupees!

Magnificent monuments

Mughal architecture reached its peak during Shah Jehan's reign. He built the famous **Taj Mahal** – a white marble mausoleum – in memory of his third wife, Mumtaz Mahal. One of the **SEVEN WONDERS OF THE WORLD**, the tomb has been described as the "embodiment of everything pure" by the poet Rudyard Kipling. Shah Jehan also commissioned other monuments such as the *Red Fort* and *Jama Masjid* in Delhi and the *Pearl Mosques* in Agra and Lahore.

Sher Shah Suri

The AFGHAN SOLDIER who defeated the mighty Mughals

By the way... I was given the title of "Sher Shah" by Bahar Khan after he saw me kill a huge tiger with my bare hands.

All about me

- **BORN:** 1486
- **DIED:** 1545
- **PLACE OF BIRTH:** Sasaram, Bihar
- **FACTOID:** I introduced a silver coin called "rupiya", which evolved into the modern rupee.
- **IN A NUTSHELL:** I revived Afghan rule in the Indian subcontinent and founded the Sur dynasty in north India.

The lion king

Born Farid Khan, Sher Shah Suri began **as a soldier in the army of Bahar Khan**, the Mughal governor of Bihar. The young Afghan impressed the governor with his *administrative and military skills* and became the ruler of Bihar after Bahar Khan's death. Sher Shah won many battles and extended his kingdom beyond Bihar. In 1539, he **DEFEATED HUMAYUN**, the Mughal Emperor, in the Battle of Chausa and became the Sultan of Delhi.

An able ruler

Sher Shah **ruled Delhi for only five years**. However, his short reign is known for good governance and a strong economy. He restored the famous **GRAND TRUNK ROAD**, which *extended from Bengal in the east to Peshawar (now in Pakistan) in the west*, and opened up trade routes with many neighbouring countries. He built a new city on the bank of Yamuna river; all that remains of the city is the Purana Qila, or Old Fort, in Delhi.

Calcutta

Sher Shah built inns and planted trees to help travellers.

Peshawar

- **BORN:** 1627
- **DIED:** 1680
- **PLACE OF BIRTH:** Shivneri, Maharashtra
- **FACTOID:** I captured more than 300 strategically important forts to protect my growing kingdom.
- **IN A NUTSHELL:** I was a Hindu king, who challenged the Mughal Empire.

Chhatrapati Shivaji
Founder of the MARATHA Kingdom

By the way... I did not have the resources to counter the large Mughal army, so I adopted guerrilla tactics and avoided confronting the enemy in open warfare.

During the coronation, his supporters hailed him as Chhatrapati, meaning the "Lord of the Universe".

Dreaming of a Hindu kingdom

Shivaji Bhonsle was born at a time when most of India was under Mughal rule, and the Deccan, the southern plateau, was governed by Muslim sultans. ***Shivaji dreamed of setting up a Hindu kingdom*** and led several military campaigns against Deccan rulers, capturing parts of their kingdoms. **Threatened by Shivaji's daring military attacks**, the Mughal Emperor Aurangzeb sent his most prominent general Jai Singh to fight him. The two rulers later signed a treaty to **END THEIR HOSTILITIES**.

Shivaji built the island fort of Underi in the Arabian Sea to keep a watch on his enemies.

Coronation of Shivaji

Although Shivaji carved out **a small Maratha kingdom for himself, with Raigad (in present-day Maharashtra) as its capital**, he lacked a formal title and was still seen as a *zamindar*, or "landlord". To address this problem, he organized ***a grand coronation to crown himself a Maratha king***. In 1674, in a lavish ceremony, with priests from Varanasi chanting holy verses from Hindu scriptures, he declared himself to be **INDEPENDENT FROM THE MUGHAL EMPIRE**.

15

Tipu Sultan

The TIGER of Mysore

By the way… as the King of Mysore, I introduced many social reforms such as prohibition of liquor consumption.

All about me

- **BORN:** 1750
- **DIED:** 1799
- **PLACE OF BIRTH:** Devanahalli, Karnataka
- **FACTOID:** I disliked the British so much that I had an automated musical toy made, showing a tiger killing a life-size European man.
- **IN A NUTSHELL:** I could have led a royal life if I had joined hands with the British, but I chose to sacrifice my life to defend the Kingdom of Mysore.

The king who defied the British

Tipu Sultan became the ruler of Mysore after the death of his father, Hyder Ali, in 1782. He was **an able administrator and a mighty warrior**, and expanded his kingdom to include parts of present-day Tamil Nadu, Karnataka, and Kerala. Aware that the British East India Company, a trading firm that colonized most of India, was eyeing his kingdom, *Tipu Sultan allied with the French Company to counter the British forces*.

The final battle between the British and Tipu took place in Seringapatam in 1799.

Tipu's throne was made of gold and set with rare diamonds and rubies.

Capture of Seringapatam

Tipu Sultan fought *four wars* against the British. He defeated his enemy in the first two, with some help in military tactics from the French – the traditional rivals of the British Empire. However, the "**Tiger of Mysore**" **suffered a setback** in the third one, losing half of his kingdom. Tipu's downfall came during the Fourth Anglo-Mysore War (1799), in which he died defending his capital **SERINGAPATAM**, in present-day Karnataka.

All about me

- **BORN:** 1835
- **DIED:** 1858
- **PLACE OF BIRTH:** Varanasi, Uttar Pradesh
- **FACTOID:** My name was changed from Manikarnika to Lakshmi Bai after my marriage to the King of Jhansi.
- **IN A NUTSHELL:** I was one of the leading figures of the First War of Independence against British rule in 1857.

Rani Lakshmi Bai

The WARRIOR Queen of Jhansi

By the way... Sir Hugh Rose, commander of the British army, was so impressed by my bravery that he compared me to Joan of Arc, the French teenager who defied the English.

The young queen

Lakshmi Bai lost her mother at **the age of four**. Raised by her father, Moropant Tombe, an official in Peshwa Baji Rao's court, Lakshmi was trained in *archery, horse riding, and martial arts*. She got married to Gangadhar Rao, the King of Jhansi, at the age of 14. In 1851, she gave birth to a son who died within three months. Later, the couple **ADOPTED A SON**, calling him Damodar Rao. Unfortunately, her husband died soon after.

Legend has it that Lakshmi Bai escaped from Jhansi by jumping her horse from the wall of her fort, with her son tied to her back.

Capture of Jhansi

After the death of the king in 1853, the British refused to acknowledge Damodar Rao as **the legal heir** to the throne of Jhansi. In 1857, they annexed the princely state, and ordered Lakshmi Bai to leave the Jhansi Fort. The queen *fought back*. She assembled an army of soldiers, including a contingent of women, to free Jhansi. Despite the initial success, her army was outmatched by the British infantry. She **DIED** fighting near Gwalior.

Mahatma Gandhi

The man who DEFIED an empire

Gandhi, an icon of peaceful resistance, pioneered non-violent methods of protest against the British government in India. He is known as the "Father of the Nation".

Early struggles

Mohandas Gandhi (1869–1948), known as **Mahatma**, or "great soul", was born in Porbandar, Gujarat. He studied law in London, England, and then spent 20 years in South Africa, joining the struggle for **BASIC RIGHTS** for Indian immigrants. He was *arrested many times*, before the government gave in to his demands. When Gandhi returned to India, he found that the British, who had ruled India as a colony since 1858, had passed strict laws to control the Indian population.

By the way...
I believe that reacting to violence with more violence is foolish. In a speech, I once said "an eye for an eye makes the whole world blind."

Did you know?
When Gandhi died, he had only 10 possessions, including a watch, sandals, spectacles, and an eating bowl.

He paved the way for...

American civil rights activist **MARTIN LUTHER KING** *(1929–1968) campaigned against* **RACIAL INEQUALITIES** *using Gandhi's non-violent methods.*

NELSON MANDELA *(1918–2013) led the struggle in South Africa to end* **APARTHEID**, *laws that kept people separate based on race. He became South Africa's first black president.*

A powerful peace

In protest against British rule in India, Gandhi started a *satyagraha*, a non-violent method of **PROTEST** that included not obeying harsh laws, boycotting British goods, and living as simple a life as possible. Gandhi attracted *millions of followers* and, in 1930, he led 50,000 people marching to the sea in protest against a new salt tax. He spent six years in prison and held a 21-day hunger strike. His ultimate aim was **Indian freedom** and self-rule.

Path to peace

Though his life was cut short, Gandhi accomplished a great deal. He helped India gain independence and end many injustices. He spoke of peace, and his life inspired many who came after him.

He gave speeches sitting at a spinning wheel to encourage people to make their own clothes and to live a simple life.

A bitter victory

In 1947, Gandhi won and India was granted *independence* from Britain. But the British split the country into two, **divided along religious lines** into Muslim Pakistan and Hindu India. This was very unpopular and **RIOTS** spread across the area. Gandhi tried to bring calm, but he was assassinated in 1948.

WEST PAKISTAN

INDIA

EAST PAKISTAN

Narmada

Tapti

Godavari

Krishna

Kaveri

Arabian Sea

Bay of Bengal

CEYLON

INDIAN OCEAN

In 1947, east Bengal chose to go with Pakistan. It later broke away from Pakistan to become Bangladesh.

The **14TH DALAI LAMA** (b. 1935) is the spiritual leader of Tibet. He lives in exile in India and campaigns for **TIBETAN INDEPENDENCE** from China.

AUNG SAN SUU KYI (b. 1945) campaigned for **DEMOCRACY** in military-ruled Myanmar and has spent 15 years under house arrest. She won the Nobel Peace Prize in 1991.

Sardar Patel

The IRON MAN of India who kept India united

All about me
- **BORN:** 1875
- **DIED:** 1950
- **PLACE OF BIRTH:** Nadiad, Gujarat
- **FACTOID:** I was the first Deputy Prime Minister of independent India.
- **IN A NUTSHELL:** People started calling me "sardar", or "leader", when I successfully led many farmers' movements in Gujarat.

Leader of the farmers

In 1918, Kheda, a district in Gujarat, faced an *acute shortage of food*, with barely enough for the poor peasants to feed themselves. At the same time, the British government wanted to increase taxes. Vallabhbhai Patel, inspired by Mahatma Gandhi, decided to take up the cause of the farming community, motivating them to **PEACEFULLY OPPOSE** the unjust decision. Encouraged by Patel, the farmers refused to pay the taxes, and **forced the government to withdraw the tariff**.

In exchange for their loyalty, the British allowed the rulers of the princely states to govern their kingdoms.

Did you know?
The Gujarat government is planning to build a 597-ft (182-m) statue of Vallabhbhai Patel, called "Statue of Unity", on the banks of the Narmada river. Once completed, it will be the world's tallest such structure.

Keeping India united

When the British granted India its freedom, they gave the princely states ruled by Maharajas and Nawabs, such as Hyderabad and Junagarh, the *option of not joining India*. Sardar Patel, India's first home minister, feared that, if exercised, this option would break the nation. Using negotiation, force, and even cunning, Patel tried every trick in his bag to make these **small kingdoms part of India**. The India as we know it today would not have been possible without his efforts.

Bose reportedly died in an air crash in 1945, although many believed he survived the crash.

All about me

- **BORN:** 1897
- **PLACE OF BIRTH:** Cuttack, Odisha
- **DIED:** 1945 (unconfirmed)
- **FACTOID:** Although I qualified for the Indian Civil Services, I refused to accept a post as a mark of my protest against the British regime.
- **IN A NUTSHELL:** I formed the Indian National Army, and led an armed struggle against the British.

A rebel is born

Like many of his peers born under the British rule, Subhas Chandra Bose too wanted to be part of the independence struggle. He joined the Congress party in 1921, but did not agree with Gandhi on many issues. A patriot, he eventually quit the party in 1939, when the Congress settled for a dominion status for India. Bose wanted complete freedom and felt it was the right time to wage an armed struggle. He formed the **FORWARD BLOC** and initiated a mass movement against British rule.

By the way... I believed in the philosophy of the *Bhagawad Gita* and always kept a pocket edition of it under my pillow.

Netaji Subhas Chandra Bose
The REVOLUTIONARY freedom fighter of the Indian independence movement

This Wanderer car was used by Bose to escape from house arrest and make his way to Peshawar, now in Pakistan.

Leading an army

The British considered **Bose a huge threat**, and placed him under house arrest in 1941. However, he escaped to Peshawar in the guise of a Pathan. From there he went to Germany, *seeking Hitler's help* to fight the British. Bose finally reached Japan. It was there that he raised **THE INDIAN NATIONAL ARMY** (INA), enlisting Indians living in Malaya, Singapore, and Myanmar. He fought the British forces in northeast India and Myanmar.

BLA7169

All about me

- **BORN:** 1879
- **DIED:** 1949
- **PLACE** ~~~~ Hyderabad, Andhra Pradesh
- **FACTO** ~~ experienced my first brush with fame as a teenager when I topped the matriculation examination conducted by Madras University.
- **IN A NUTSHELL:** I decided to join the freedom struggle against the British after the Partition of Bengal in 1905.

BOYCOTT BRITISH GOODS

A poet is born

Sarojini Naidu started writing poetry from a very young age. She was only 13 when she wrote a **1300-line long poem**, *The Lady of the Lake,* during a school break. So impressed was the Nizam of Hyderabad with the young poetess that he gave her a scholarship to study in England. Her poetry collections *The **Golden Threshold**, **The Bird of Time**,* and ***The Broken Wing*** attracted a huge Indian and English readership, earning her the title of **NIGHTINGALE OF INDIA**.

By the way...
after India became independent, I served as the first Governor of the United Provinces (now Uttar Pradesh), and also contributed to the drafting of the Indian Constitution.

In 1930, Sarojini actively participated in the Dandi March, led by Gandhi.

Leading from the front

While in England, Sarojini Naidu was drawn to Mahatma Gandhi's non-violent struggle in India. Back home, Sarojini went around the country making *fiery speeches*, inspiring people to join the independence struggle. She later joined the Congress party, and was instrumental in having a resolution passed that **allowed women to have voting rights**. In 1925, she became the **first Indian woman Congress president**. She played a key role in the Non-cooperation Movement (1920), and Quit India Movement (1942).

Sarojini Naidu
The NIGHTINGALE of India

BR Ambedkar

The man who waged a relentless struggle for the RIGHTS OF DALITS

All about me

- **BORN:** 1891
- **DIED:** 1956
- **PLACE OF BIRTH:** Mhow, Madhya Pradesh
- **FACTOID:** I was the first person from the Mahar community of "untouchables" to complete higher education.
- **IN A NUTSHELL:** I fought for the equal rights of "untouchables", and played a key role in drafting the Constitution of independent India.

By the way... in the later part of my life, I converted to Buddhism as I felt it was a religion that advocated equality among people.

Ambedkar included Article 17 in the Constitution to abolish untouchability in India.

Constitution of India

Son of a lesser god

As a young boy in school, Bhimrao Ramji Ambedkar was not allowed to sit next to children from higher castes or drink water from the same tap as them. Despite facing many such humiliations, he excelled as a student and **won a scholarship to pursue higher studies in the USA**. Upon his return to India, Ambedkar became politically active, raising his *voice against all forms of social injustice*. He launched several movements to fight untouchability and demanded a **SEPARATE ELECTORATE** for "untouchables", or Dalits.

A preliminary conference was held by all parties to work out a new Constitution for India.

Father of the Constitution

Bhimrao Ambedkar was the **first law minister** of independent India. Appointed the *Chairman of the Drafting Committee*, Ambedkar oversaw the writing of the new Constitution. He introduced many rights such as **freedom of religion** and civil liberties, and outlawed all forms of **DISCRIMINATION**.

23

Jawaharlal Nehru

India's first PRIME MINISTER

Jawaharlal Nehru grew up in an India ruled by the British. A committed patriot, Nehru not only helped India gain freedom but was also among its first few modern leaders.

Early life

Jawaharlal Nehru (1889–1964) was born in Allahabad, Uttar Pradesh. His father, Moti Lal Nehru, was a wealthy lawyer and a well-known political activist. At the age of 16, Nehru went to Harrow, a leading school in England, where he studied for two years. Later, he read law at the **Inner Temple, London**. However, Nehru's heart was not in the profession. This was a time when people in India were raising their voice against the British regime, and young Nehru was very keen to join this fight.

Young Nehru posing with his parents.

Did you know?
An animal lover, Nehru kept a private zoo at his residence. His pets included deer, crocodiles, tiger cubs, pigeons, dogs, and squirrels.

Nehru played an active role during India's civil disobedience movement in the pre–independence era.

The patriot

Inspired by Gandhi, Nehru joined the Indian National Congress, the party at the forefront of the independence struggle. Elected as the Congress president in 1929, Nehru **opposed the earlier Congress leaders who believed in petitioning the British**. Instead, he pushed for non-cooperation with the British and **COMPLETE INDEPENDENCE**.

He couldn't have done it without...

HAROLD LASKI *(1861–1931) was a British political theorist who greatly* **BELIEVED IN SOCIALISM**. *Laski deeply influenced Nehru in shaping modern India.*

MAHATMA GANDHI *(1869–1948) was Nehru's political mentor. It was under Gandhi's guidance that Nehru emerged as the* **FOREMOST LEADER** *of the freedom struggle.*

Maker of modern India

After India won its freedom in August 1947, Jawaharlal Nehru took over as its **first Prime Minister**. He is still remembered for his **famous speech (Tryst with Destiny)** on the eve of Independence Day. Nehru wanted India to become a modern nation. He borrowed the best ideas from around the world to make this happen. He favoured a **mixed economy**, where both the government and the private sector participated in India's development. He also believed in an India where people of all religious faiths lived together in harmony.

At the stroke of the midnight hour...

A man of letters

Jawaharlal Nehru wrote a number of books, such as **The Discovery of India** and **Letters from a Father to his Daughter**. To promote literature, he established the **Sahitya Academy** and **National Book Trust** – two Indian institutions committed to publishing quality books in English and other Indian languages.

By the way...
the "Nehru Jacket", a closed-neck coat-like garment worn by me, became so popular that it has been listed among the "top 10 global political fashion statements" by *Time* magazine.

"Chacha Nehru"

Nehru often said that children were like flower buds in a garden. They should be lovingly nurtured, as they are the real strength of a country. Children loved him, too, and called him "Chacha Nehru" affectionately. Nehru's birthday, 14 November, is celebrated all over India as Children's Day.

He paved the way for...

Nehru played a crucial role in the **NON-ALIGNED MOVEMENT**. *It was started in 1961 by a group of nations that did not want to side with either* **THE USA** OR **USSR**, *two powerful nations then at loggerheads with each other.*

Nehru set up the **PLANNING COMMISSION OF INDIA** *in 1950. Its role is to formulate the* "**FIVE-YEAR PLANS**", *and perform a host of other economic functions.*

Jayaprakash Narayan

The REBEL leader of the masses

All about me

- **BORN:** 1902
- **DIED:** 1979
- **PLACE OF BIRTH:** Sitabdiara, Bihar
- **FACTOID:** I was popularly referred to as the "Lok Nayak" ("people's hero").
- **IN A NUTSHELL:** I am known for forming the Congress Socialist Party in pre-independence India and for leading the Bihar Movement in the 1970s.

The firebrand socialist

Jayaprakash Narayan, also known as JP, was **influenced by communist ideas** floated by German philosopher Karl Marx (1818–1883) during his stay in the USA. On his return to India in 1929, *he joined the struggle for India's independence*, and went to jail on several occasions for defying the British. In 1934, JP and his friends formed a **SOCIALIST WING within the Congress party** to steer it towards socialism. After independence, JP **retired from active politics** and dedicated himself to the **Sarvodaya Movement**, or the "progress of all" to strengthen Indian democracy.

By the way... I worked as a fruit picker, jam packer, waiter, mechanic, and salesman to pay for my studies in the USA.

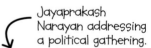

Jayaprakash Narayan addressing a political gathering.

Total revolution

In 1974, JP led the Bihar Movement against the corrupt government of the state. It soon grew into a campaign against the Congress party, which ruled the country then, but faced serious corruption charges. Addressing a mammoth crowd in Patna, JP declared, "... we don't just want a change of government... **we want total revolution**." In 1975, he called for Indira Gandhi, then Prime Minister, to resign, after she was found guilty of flouting election rules. Instead, she clamped a national emergency and jailed JP and other opposition leaders. She was defeated in the next general elections in 1977.

All about me

- **BORN:** 1917
- **DIED:** 1984
- **PLACE OF BIRTH:** Allahabad, Uttar Pradesh
- **FACTOID:** Born as Indira Priyadarshini Nehru, I was the only child of the former prime minister Jawaharlal Nehru.
- **IN A NUTSHELL:** I was the Indian prime minister during 1966–1977 and 1980–1984.

Indira Gandhi

India's first WOMAN prime minister

Political heir

Indira Gandhi became the prime minister of India when Jawaharlal Nehru's successor, **LAL BAHADUR SHASTRI**, died unexpectedly in 1966. *This was a critical time in India's history* – the 1965 Indo-Pak war had just ended and the nation was facing a **severe food shortage, prices were rising, and there were not enough jobs**. Indira Gandhi showed a lot of grit and determination in dealing with the problems at hand, and surprised her opponents who were not expecting much from her.

The "Iron Lady" of India

She **nationalized (brought under the control of government) 14 leading banks**, making the **availability of credit** to agriculture and small-scale industries easy. Indira Gandhi led from the front when India went to war against Pakistan in 1971, in support of Bangladesh's fight for freedom. But her popularity took a beating when she declared *a state of emergency* in the country in 1975–1977. She ruled like a dictator during this time, taking away all fundamental rights of citizens and not allowing newspapers to report against her. Her life was cut short tragically when two of her bodyguards **SHOT HER DEAD** inside her home in 1984.

By the way... I married Feroze Gandhi (no relative of Mahatma Gandhi), a freedom fighter and member of parliament, in 1942.

JRD Tata

India's first pilot and the man who pioneered AVIATION in India

By the way...
I provided the necessary financial support to Dr Homi Bhabha to establish the Institute of Fundamental Research in Mumbai.

This business tycoon had the courage and ability to convert hurdles into opportunities.

Early life

Jehangir Ratanji Dadabhoy Tata (1904–1993), also known as JRD, was born to a French mother and Parsi father. He was educated in France, Japan, and England, and **served in the French army for a year**. JRD wanted to continue his services in the army, but his father, Ratanji Dadabhoy Tata, **brought him back** to India to *carry forward the Tata business legacy*.

India gets wings

As a young boy, JRD was inspired by French aviator and inventor Louis Bleriot, and started taking a great interest in flying. In 1929, he became the **first Indian to clear the test for pilots**. Not stopping at this, JRD became instrumental in setting up **INDIA'S FIRST AIRLINE SERVICE**, the Tata Airlines, now known as Air India. In 1932, JRD piloted the airlines' inaugural flight between Karachi and Bombay (now Mumbai).

Did you know?
I was so fond of flying a plane that even at the age of 70 I piloted my own aircraft from Mumbai to London.

He couldn't have done it without...

*JRD Tata's uncle by relation, **JAMSHEDJI TATA** (1839–1904) was the founder of the Tata Group. He was the first person to show the world that big businesses could be set up in India too.*

LOUIS BLERIOT (1872–1936) was a French aviator and engineer, who gave wings to JRD Tata's flying dreams. Bleriot was the first person to cross the English Channel in an aircraft.

Bombay House, the historical building in Mumbai, is the head office of the Tata Group.

Taking the Tata legacy forward

In 1938, at the age of 34, **JRD became the head of Tata Sons**, the largest industrial group in India. Under his leadership, **TATA SONS REACHED NEW HEIGHTS**, growing from a group of 14 enterprises to a conglomerate of 95 companies. JRD was the founder of many big brands and companies of today, such as the Tata Consultancy Services, Tata Motors, Titan, Tata Tea, and Voltas. He was a visionary who dreamed of **building a self-sufficient and modern India**.

A benevolent boss

JRD Tata cared greatly for his employees. Tata Steel, under JRD's leadership, was the first company to have policies such as an eight-hour working day, free medical aid, workers' provident fund, and accident compensation, which were later adopted as compulsory requirements in India.

He paved the way for...

The Tata Airlines paved the way for the **AVIATION INDUSTRY IN INDIA**. Not just limited to domestic services, India's first international air carrier, Air India International, was also a product of the Tata Group.

JRD founded the **TATA INSTITUTE OF FUNDAMENTAL RESEARCH** in Mumbai in 1945 – an institute geared to carry out basic research in physics, chemistry, biology, mathematics, and computer science.

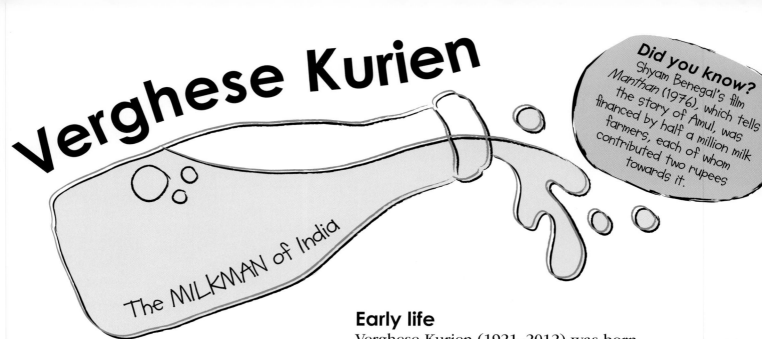

Verghese Kurien

The MILKMAN of India

Early life

Verghese Kurien (1921–2012) was born in Kozhikode, Kerala. He graduated in physics from **Loyola College**, Chennai, in 1940. A bright student, Kurien won a government of India **SCHOLARSHIP** to do his **master's in dairy engineering** from Michigan State University, USA.

From engineer to milkman

Upon his return from the USA in 1949, Kurien was asked to work at a government creamery in Anand, Gujarat, in exchange for the scholarship he had received. Disgusted with the way the creamery was run, Kurien was ready to pack his bag and leave, when **Tribhuvandas Patel**, a freedom fighter and well-wisher of farmers, persuaded him to stay back. Patel had set up a farmers' union called the Kaira District Cooperative Milk Producers Union Limited, to help farmers get better prices, and wanted Kurien to join him. The two came together to set up a new milk processing plant, which later came to be **KNOWN AS AMUL**.

He paved the way for...

Kurien set up the **INSTITUTE OF RURAL MANAGEMENT (IRMA)** *in Anand in 1979. It is an institute that trains students in* **RURAL DEVELOPMENT.**

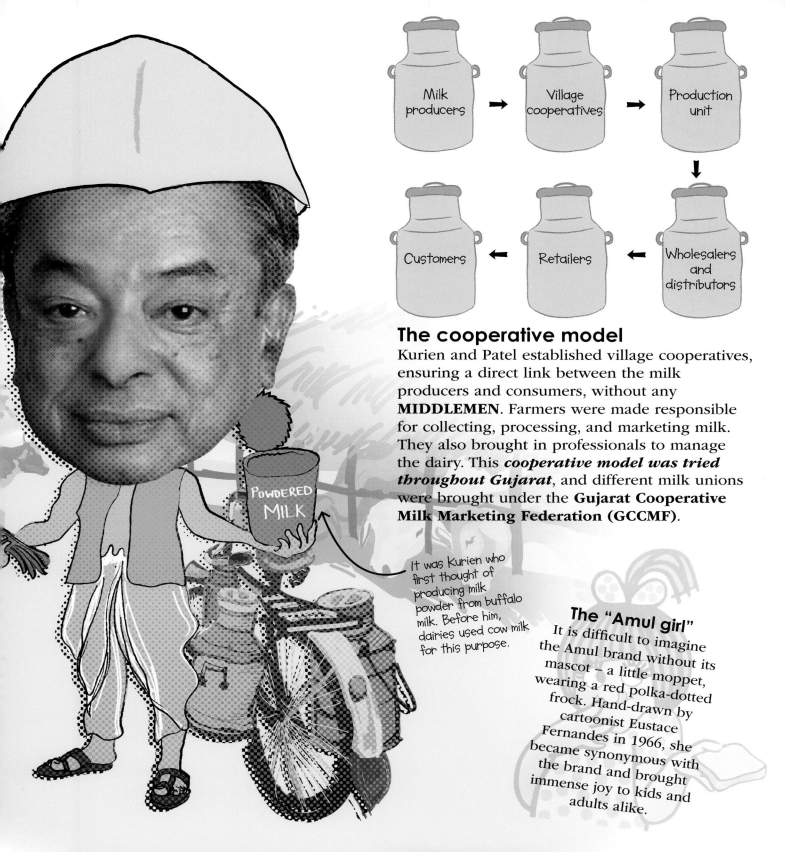

Milk producers → Village cooperatives → Production unit

↓

Customers ← Retailers ← Wholesalers and distributors

The cooperative model

Kurien and Patel established village cooperatives, ensuring a direct link between the milk producers and consumers, without any **MIDDLEMEN**. Farmers were made responsible for collecting, processing, and marketing milk. They also brought in professionals to manage the dairy. This *cooperative model was tried throughout Gujarat*, and different milk unions were brought under the **Gujarat Cooperative Milk Marketing Federation (GCCMF)**.

POWDERED MILK

It was Kurien who first thought of producing milk powder from buffalo milk. Before him, dairies used cow milk for this purpose.

The "Amul girl"

It is difficult to imagine the Amul brand without its mascot – a little moppet, wearing a red polka-dotted frock. Hand-drawn by cartoonist Eustace Fernandes in 1966, she became synonymous with the brand and brought immense joy to kids and adults alike.

With a view to replicate the Amul model across India, Kurien established the **NATIONAL DAIRY DEVELOPMENT BOARD (NDDB)** IN **1965**.

Kurien is known as the "Father of the **WHITE REVOLUTION**" in India. Thanks to him, India is now the world's largest producer of milk.

E Sreedharan

The METRO MAN of India

Government projects are known to take forever to complete, but E Sreedharan proved otherwise by delivering projects before time and within the allotted budget.

Known for leading a disciplined life, Sreedharan wakes up at 4:30am every day.

By the way...
I was presented the Railway Minister's Award in 1963, the Padma Shri in 2001, and the Lokmanya Tilak Award in 2013.

Ahead of time

Elattuvalapil Sreedharan (b. 1932) was born in a village in Kerala. He graduated as an ***engineer*** from a college in Andhra Pradesh and joined the Southern Railway in 1954. Sreedharan landed his first major project in 1964, when he was asked to rebuild the **Pamban Bridge** that connected Rameswaram, an island city, with mainland Tamil Nadu. The bridge had been washed away in a cyclone, leaving the people of Rameswaram stranded. Sreedharan was given six months to complete the work – he **FINISHED THE JOB IN 45 DAYS**.

He paved the way for...

The SUCCESS OF THE DELHI METRO has inspired other states to introduce the metro transport system in their cities, such as BENGALURU in Karnataka and KOCHI in Kerala.

Moving mountains

Sreedharan was due to retire in 1990, when he was given the herculean task of building the **KONKAN RAILWAY** in the hilly terrain of the **Western Ghats**. He was given eight years to complete the project that involved *blasting mountains, digging tunnels, building bridges, and laying 760km (472 miles) of rail tracks* between Mumbai and Kochi. Sreedharan finished the project in seven years.

The biggest challenge came from the bridges that had to be built over soft soil.

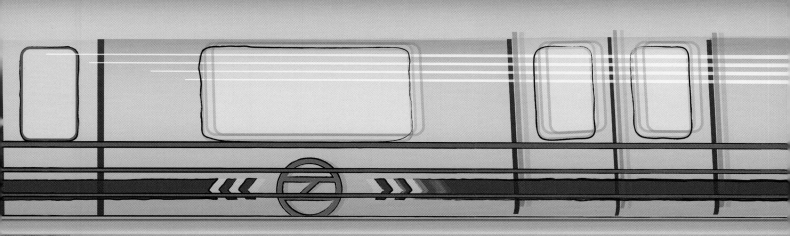

The Delhi Metro revolution

In mid-2005, Sreedharan, already 75, was appointed the **Managing Director** of the Delhi Metro. Like all his earlier projects, Sreedharan finished this one too *well ahead of schedule*, and changed the way people of Delhi travelled from one part of the city to another. Today, the **DELHI METRO** compares with the best transport systems the world has to offer.

54

Metro pillar numbers are now used to locate addresses in Delhi.

Marvellous metro

The Delhi Metro carries 2.2 million people every day and earns Rs 4 crore a day. The world over, a metro train is considered late if it is delayed by two minutes or more. For the Delhi Metro, this is one minute, and it has been punctual 99.97 per cent of the time.

NR Narayana Murthy

This man showed that a large and successful business can be set up without bending rules.

Starting from scratch

Narayana Murthy (b. 1946) was born to *educated but poor parents* in Mysore, Karnataka. As a young boy, he had no money, no family backing, but just a *dogged determination and faith* in what he believed was the **FUTURE OF BUSINESS**. After completing his studies, he took up his first job at the Indian Institute of Management, Ahmedabad. Although he earned a **meagre salary**, he considers this phase of life to be the best as he got to learn what engineering was all about. Later, he joined Patni Computer Systems in Pune as the chief systems programmer. It is here that the idea of Infosys took root.

By the way...
Infosys did not own a computer in its first two years of existence. The company started operations while waiting for permission to import a computer.

He couldn't have done it without...

SUDHA MURTHY (b.1950), *Narayana Murthy's wife, is a social worker and author. It was her savings that were instrumental in the founding of Infosys.*

The Infosys story

In 1981, Murthy **borrowed Rs 10,000** from his wife and started Infosys with six other partners. Under his leadership, Infosys became **ONE OF THE LARGEST INFORMATION TECHNOLOGY (IT) COMPANIES** of India, providing business services and solutions worldwide. It became the first Indian company to be listed on NASDAQ (the American Stock Exchange). He was the CEO of Infosys from 1981–2002, and served as the chairman of the board from 2002–2011, retiring in 2011. However, in 2013, he **returned to Infosys** as its executive chairman and additional director.

This is the Global Education Centre of Infosys in Mysore. It is the world's largest corporate training institute, where new recruits and potential employees are trained.

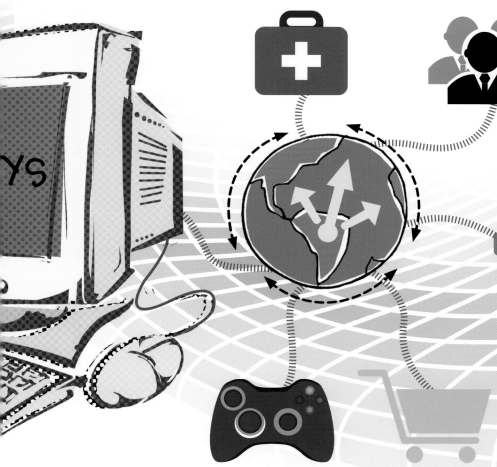

Did you know? In 1976, Murthy started a company called Softronics. This venture, however failed to take off.

Accolades keep flowing

Narayana Murthy has received many awards, both national and international. *Forbes* magazine listed him as one of the greatest entrepreneurs of all time, alongside Steve Jobs and Bill Gates. The Government of India awarded him the Padma Shri in 2000, for his contribution to the country's IT sector, and the Padma Vibhushan, India's second highest civilian award, in 2008.

He paved the way for...

NANDAN NILEKANI *(b.1955), co-founder of Infosys and one of India's leading entrepreneurs, started his IT career with Patni Computer Systems, where he met and was interviewed by Narayana Murthy.*

*Infosys set **GLOBAL STANDARDS FOR INDIAN BUSINESSES**, showing that the best IT businesses could be run as efficiently in India as anywhere else. It proved that an Indian company can be bench-marked alongside top global companies.*

All about me

- **BORN:** 1933
- **PLACE OF BIRTH:** Ahmedabad, Gujarat
- **FACTOID:** I won many prestigious awards such as the Indira Gandhi Prize and Ramon Magsaysay Award.
- **IN A NUTSHELL:** I set up India's largest trade union for working women to fight for their rights.

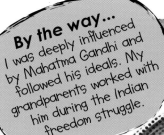

By the way... I was deeply influenced by Mahatma Gandhi and followed his ideals. My grandparents worked with him during the Indian freedom struggle.

Ela Bhatt

The GENTLE REVOLUTIONARY who works for the empowerment of poor, self-employed women

SEWA Cooperative Bank

The invisible women

While working as a lawyer with the Textile Labour Association in Gujarat, Ela Bhatt found that despite working hard in the factory, women workers had **NO RIGHTS**. The **young lawyer** was disturbed by the fact that contractors exploited the poor women – paying them low wages, since there were *no laws protecting* them. She found out that although 80 per cent women were economically active, they did not have the power to ask for higher wages.

SEWA has developed a rich pool of embroidery by artisans from all over India.

Better income, better lives

In 1972, Ela Bhatt set up the ***Self-Employed Women's Association*** (***SEWA***) in Gujarat to fight for better pay and working conditions for women. More than **1.2 million poor women** joined SEWA, setting up an example for the world to follow. In 1974, Bhatt helped form a cooperative bank to provide **SMALL LOANS** to women to start businesses. With time, SEWA started providing legal services and child-care facilities to women workers.

All about me

■ **BORN:** 1953
■ **PLACE OF BIRTH:** Bengaluru, Karnataka
■ **FACTOID:** Apart from being the head of Biocon, I am currently also the chairperson of the Indian Institute of Management, Bengaluru.
■ **IN A NUTSHELL:** I am a self-made entrepreneur who proved that women, too, can run successful businesses.

By the way... I am part of the Prime Minister's Council on Trade & Industry in India and the US–India CEO Forum.

Breaking the stereotype

Kiran Mazumdar Shaw started working with Biocon Biochemicals Limited, a biotechnology firm based in Ireland, in 1978. Later that year **SHE FOUNDED BIOCON IN INDIA** with an initial capital of only Rs 10,000. It was a difficult road to walk on – the banks were hesitant to give her a loan, as no one had heard of *biotechnology* (using micro-organisms, such as bacteria, to create useful products), and it was rare for a **woman to lead a company in India in those days**. She even had difficulty hiring people to work for her.

Biocon reaches the top

The initial lack of support and limited resources did not discourage Shaw. She built a company that became one of the leading biotechnology firms. Biocon is known for making low-cost drugs and delivering affordable medical products to partners in 70 countries. The company has created a name for itself globally, and has made **SHAW, ITS MANAGING DIRECTOR**, among the 100 most powerful women in the world.

Kiran Mazumdar Shaw

A successful BUSINESSWOMAN who is also one of the RICHEST

Thinkers

When these brainy Indians put on their thinking caps, they came up with some new and very influential ideas. Some tried to figure out how the world works, while others decided to do something about suffering and injustice. Whether philosophers, religious leaders, human rights activists, or conservationists, these trailblazers all gave us something to think about.

Religious leaders

New INSIGHTS into the meaning of life

The teachings of the Buddha, Mahavira, Shankaracharya, and Guru Nanak have had a huge impact on human history and the lives of billions of people.

Gautam Buddha
(c. 563–483BCE)

Growing up in a palace in modern-day Nepal, Gautam discovered that the world was filled with the old, sick, and dying. He set out to *find the answer to human suffering*. He experienced "enlightenment" under a Bodhi Tree in Gaya, in present-day Bihar. His followers, the **BUDDHISTS**, live a life of **kindness and morality**, detached from material desires.

The wheel represents the eightfold path of Buddhism. ⇨

Lord Mahavira
(c. 599–527BCE)

Mahavira, also known as Vardhaman, was the *last tirthankara, or the "enlightened one"*, of Jain tradition. He was born a prince in present-day Bihar. At the age of 30, he left the royal palace and gave up all possessions to become a monk. He spent the next 12 years in intense meditation **to overcome wordly temptations**. His message of **NON-VIOLENCE, TRUTH,** and **NON-POSSESSION** attracted a large following in India.

The hand with a wheel signifies the Jain vow of ahimsa. ⇨

Adi Shankaracharya
(c. 788–820CE)

Shankaracharya was born in present-day Kerala, but there is no clarity about his birth and death years. He was known to be a gifted child who interpreted *the ancient Hindu scriptures, such as the Vedas and Upanishads* by the time he was 15, and became the leading authority in yoga by the age of 20. Shankaracharya established **CENTRES OF LEARNING THROUGHOUT INDIA** to help human beings overcome suffering through wisdom and meditation.

⬅ Om is a sacred Hindu sound that embodies the essence of the entire universe.

Guru Nanak
(1469–1539CE)

Born as a Hindu in Nankana Sahib, in modern-day Pakistan, Guru Nanak *sought the truth about God from an early age*. He had an experience that he described as being taken to the court of God. He then set out to teach people that a **profound awareness of God** was more important than the customs of religions. The Guru expressed all his teachings in Punjabi to reach the masses. His followers – **SIKHS** – are spread all across India.

⬆ The Khanda symbolizes God's universal and creative power.

Poets of Faith

Speaking the language of POETRY and MUSIC

The selfless lives and inspiring verses of these poets taught millions of people to transcend social barriers and love everyone.

Amir Khusro
(1253–1325)

A **Sufi musician and poet**, Amir Khusro has had a tremendous influence on Indian music and culture. Regarded as the "*father of qawwali*" (devotional Sufi music), Khusro **ENRICHED HINDUSTANI CLASSICAL MUSIC** by introducing Persian and Arabic elements in it. His music was based on the **Sufi teaching** that **union with God** can be achieved through prayers alone, regardless of a person's religious or social standing.

All his life, Kabir worked as a weaver in Benaras (Varanasi).

Kabir
(c.1440–1518)

According to a legend, Kabir was born to a Hindu widow, but adopted by a childless Muslim weaver couple. **Spiritually inclined**, the poet-saint combined the tenets of Hindu Vaishnava and the Muslim Sufi traditions in his teachings. He **opposed the caste system** and believed in *equality of all*. His *dohas*, or "couplets", explain his teachings with examples from everyday life.

Surdas
(c.1483–1563)

Blind poet Surdas is known for his **loving description of Lord Krishna's life** in a folk language called "Brajbhasa". It remains a mystery to this day, how a blind poet could present Lord Krishna's childhood in such *vivid and colourful detail*. Through his verses, Surdas taught people to **SHUN THEIR CASTE PREJUDICES**, and simply express their love for God.

Depictions of Surdas show him playing the wooden manjira with one hand while singing his bhajans (devotional songs).

Surdas spent the last years of his life in Braj, the land of Krishna.

Mirabai
(1498–1547)

Mirabai was born a princess. She lost her husband at an early age, but refused to immolate herself on her husband's funeral pyre, as the custom demanded. Instead, she chose to devote her life to the **WORSHIP OF LORD KRISHNA**. She showed that the relationship between God and man is one of **love and worship, rather than of rituals and customs**.

Playing her ektara, a one-stringed instrument, Mirabai sang the hundreds of bhajans she composed – all devoted to Krishna.

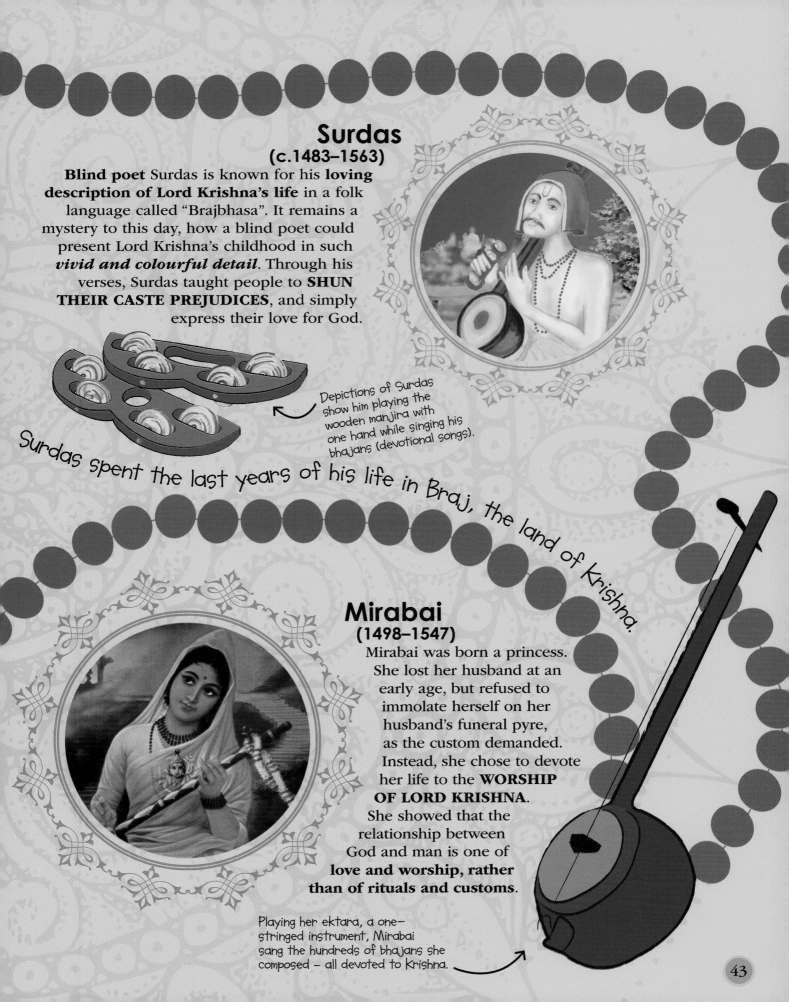

43

Raja Ram Mohan Roy

The MAKER of modern India

This social reformer raised his voice against the orthodox Hindu culture in the early 1800s.

Early life

Ram Mohan Roy (1772–1833) was born in Radhanagar in British-ruled Bengal. This was a period when the people of Bengal were challenging some of the existing superstitious beliefs and customs. Inspired by some of these ideas, young Ram Mohan started *questioning the ills of Hindu society*, and set his mind on making religious reforms.

By the way...
I mastered several languages, including Sanskrit, Persian, and Arabic, at the age of 15, and later learned Hebrew, Greek, and English as well.

The social crusader

As a young man, Roy was horrified to see his sister-in-law immolate herself on her husband's funeral pyre. Shaken to the core, he wrote several letters to the British government, petitioning them to **BAN THE BARBARIC CUSTOM OF SATI**. His efforts bore fruit when Governor-General Lord Bentinck passed a law **abolishing sati** in 1929. Not stopping at this, Roy strove against *child marriage* and supported the *remarriage of widows*. In 1829, **he founded the Brahmo Samaj** to fight religious orthodoxy and caste rigidity.

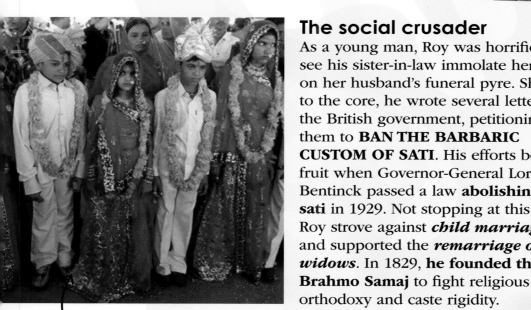

Although the Indian government has banned child marriage, it is still common in certain parts of India, where children are married off at a very young age.

He paved the way for...

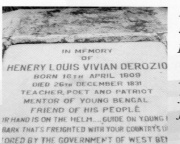

IN MEMORY OF
HENERY LOUIS VIVIAN DEROZIO
BORN 18TH APRIL 1809
DIED 26TH DECEMBER 1831
TEACHER, POET AND PATRIOT
MENTOR OF YOUNG BENGAL
FRIEND OF HIS PEOPLE
IR HAND IS ON THE HELM... GUIDE ON YOUNG I
BARK THAT'S FREIGHTED WITH YOUR COUNTRY'S D
ORED BY THE GOVERNMENT OF WEST BEI

Inspired by Ram Mohan Roy's social reform movement, famous poet **HENRY VIVIAN DEROZIO** *(1809–1831) started the Young Bengal Movement, motivating young people in Bengal to think freely and rationally.*

- ✗ SATI
- ✗ POLYGAMY
- ✗ CHILD MARRIAGE
- ✗ FEMALE INFANTICIDE
- ✗ CASTE DISCRIMINATION
- ✓ RIGHT TO PROPERTY FOR WOMEN
- ✗ IDOL WORSHIP
- ✓ ENGLISH EDUCATION
- ✓ FREE SPEECH

Ram Mohan Roy's movement covered religious, social, economic, educational, political, and national issues.

Broadening the horizon

Ram Mohan Roy **pushed for a new education system** in India to break the shackles of religious superstition. He favoured a more **LIBERAL SYSTEM OF LEARNING**, which **included subjects such as English, mathematics, chemistry, and anatomy**. Along with the Scottish scholar David Hare and the Scottish missionary Alexander Duff, he **established the Hindu College in Calcutta** in 1817. In 1825, he founded the Vedanta College, which offered courses that combined traditional Indian learning with Western scientific studies.

Did you know?
Businessman Dwarkanath Tagore built a tomb in honour of Raja Ram Mohan Roy in Bristol, England, in 1843.

Freedom of the press
Ram Mohan Roy was a supporter of free speech and expression and fought for the rights of the vernacular press. In those days, news articles had to be approved by the British government before being published. Roy protested against this control and argued that truth should not be suppressed simply because the government did not like it.

DADABHAI NAOROJI (1825–1917), one of the most prominent political leaders of the Indian freedom struggle, carried forward the tradition of liberal political and social thinking, as shown by Ram Mohan Roy.

Much influenced by Ram Mohan Roy, **SWAMI VIVEKANANDA** (1863–1902) also tried to unite the West with the East, keeping the best of both worlds. He claimed himself to have taken up the task Roy had set out to do.

Swami Vivekananda

The MONK who took Indian spirituality to the Western world

All about me

- **BORN:** 1863
- **DIED:** 1902
- **PLACE OF BIRTH:** Kolkata
- **FACTOID:** My parents named me Narendra Nath Dutta. I came to be known as Swami Vivekananda when I became a "sanyasi", or monk.
- **IN A NUTSHELL:** I showed the world that religion and science can exist together.

The Vivekananda Rock Memorial was built in 1970 in Kanyakumari, Tamil Nadu.

Search for truth

From a very young age, Vivekananda was eager to know the ***truth about God*** – he often questioned people about whether they had seen God. While in college, he met the great spiritual teacher **Sri Ramakrishna Paramahamsa**, who helped him clear his doubts about the existence of God. He accepted Ramakrishna as his guru and under his guidance became a sage. Vivekananda spread the message of **LOVE AND HUMANITY**, travelling all over India as a wandering monk.

By the way... In Kanyakumari, I meditated continuously for three days. The place where I sat is now a popular tourist spot called Vivekananda Rock.

The journey to the West

In 1893, Vivekananda visited Chicago to represent Hinduism at the **World's Parliament of Religions**. His ***flawless oratory*** on Hinduism **wowed the Western world**, catapulting him to the status of a world leader. His vast knowledge of Eastern and Western culture as well as his deep ***spiritual insight into world religions*** appealed to all. He knew India was a land of spirituality and religion, while the West had progressed in science. Vivekananda believed a **HEALTHY SYNTHESIS OF THE EAST AND WEST**, of religion and science, would benefit society.

All about me

- **BORN:** 1918
- **PLACE OF BIRTH:** Bellur, Karnataka
- **FACTOID:** In 2004, I was named one of the "100 Most Influential People" by *Time* magazine.
- **IN A NUTSHELL:** My yoga is the most widely practised form of yoga in Europe and the USA.

From sick to fit

Born during an influenza epidemic in Bellur, Bellur Krishnamachar Sundararaja Iyengar was a **SICKLY** and **WEAK CHILD**. When he was 15, his brother-in-law T Krishnamacharya – an accomplished yoga teacher – called him to Mysore. Regular practice of **yoga asanas**, or "postures", improved Iyengar's health greatly. In 1937, at the age of 18, he moved to Pune to teach yoga at the Deccan Gymkhana Club. He spent many hours perfecting the *asanas*, which helped him **set up his own yoga school later**.

By the way... the Oxford English Dictionary has added my name, "Iyengar", to its word list.

BKS Iyengar

The master yogi who introduced YOGA to the world

Iyengar's Salamba sirsasana (headstand pose) is one of the most popular postures among practitioners of yoga in the West.

Iyengar encourages the use of props, such as foam bricks, to help people do the asanas easily.

The world follows the yogi

In 1952, Iyengar met **violinist Yehudi Menuhin**, who introduced him to the Western world. Menuhin arranged for Iyengar to teach in the UK, Switzerland, France, and other parts of the world. During his international tours, he taught yoga to some well-known people, such as the Queen Mother of Belgium, who further popularized his form of yoga. In 1966, he wrote his first book, *Light on Yoga*, which became an **INTERNATIONAL BESTSELLER** and has since been translated into 18 languages.

By the way...
I was responsible for introducing several changes in the Tamil alphabet and the language in general.

All about me

- **BORN:** 1879
- **DIED:** 1973
- **PLACE OF BIRTH:** Erode, Tamil Nadu
- **FACTOID:** My real name was Erode Venkata Ramasamy. Periyar, a name given to me by my followers, means the "respected one" in Tamil.
- **IN A NUTSHELL:** I worked hard to eradicate inequality of castes from Tamil society.

For an equal society

Periyar believed all men and women are equal, and *fought against caste-based discrimination in Tamil society*. He spearheaded movements such as the **VAIKOM SATYAGRAHA**, in 1924–1925, to protest against untouchability and allow Dalits to enter temples. He also started the **SELF-RESPECT MOVEMENT** in 1925, to seek a life of dignity and respect for non-Brahmin backward castes. He opposed religion strongly and believed that priests and other men of religion invent **myths and superstitions to deceive** innocent people.

Periyar Ramasamy

The SOCIAL REFORMER who fought for the dignity of backward castes

Freedom of language

In 1937, the provincial government wanted to enforce **compulsory teaching of Hindi** in schools in Tamil Nadu. Periyar opposed this *forceful imposition* and launched a series of anti-Hindi agitations, forcing the government to withdraw the policy in 1940. Currently, every state in India has the **RIGHT TO USE ITS OWN LANGUAGE** or English for official communication.

All about me

- **BORN:** 1888
- **DIED:** 1975
- **PLACE OF BIRTH:** Tiruttani, Andhra Pradesh
- **FACTOID:** I was the first Vice President and the second President of India.
- **IN A NUTSHELL:** My father wanted me to be a priest, but I chose to be a teacher and philosopher.

Sarvepalli Radhakrishnan

The famous TEACHER who later became the President of India

A much-loved teacher

Dr S Radhakrishnan was a **brilliant student**, and most of his studies were funded through scholarships. He became an *Assistant Professor of Philosophy* in Madras Presidency College at the age of 21. His mastery of the subject and his clarity of thought and expression made him a **sought-after teacher**. To honour his contributions as a teacher, Oxford University set up scholarship in 1989 called the Radhakrishnan Chevening Scholarships.

The philosopher-President

Dr Radhakrishnan was already a well-known teacher and philosopher when he was elected the first Vice President of India in 1952. He was a great scholar of *Hindu philosophy* (Vedanta), and for him, philosophy was a **way of understanding life**. He went on to become the President in 1962. Bertrand Russell, the British philosopher, hailed his appointment as "an honour to Philosophy... and a tribute to India".

By the way... my birthday, 5 September, is celebrated all over India as Teachers' Day.

Aurobindo Ghose

The NATIONALIST leader who later became a SPIRITUAL TEACHER

From politics to spirituality

Aurobindo Ghose was born to well-educated and rich parents. At the age of nine, **he went to England** and studied in Manchester, London, and Cambridge, where he excelled as a student. Back in India in 1903, he **joined the ongoing freedom struggle**. He played a pivotal role in the anti-British movements in Bengal, and strongly *resisted the partition of Bengal*. In 1908, he was jailed for a year on suspicion of being involved in a bomb plot, during which **he had mystical experiences**.

Auroville is an all-inclusive model town, where people from all communities can live together in peace and harmony.

The Matrimandir, a meditation facility in Auroville, is considered the "soul of the city".

Auroville

GUESTS

Power of yoga

In 1910, Aurobindo came to **PONDICHERRY**. By this time, he had withdrawn from politics and started focusing his energies on **attaining spirituality through yoga** and meditation. He combined the essence of the major schools of yoga and came up with what is known as **integral yoga**.

By the way...
I founded the Sri Aurobindo Ashram in Pondicherry in 1926, with the help of a French woman Mirra Alfassa who later came to be known as the Mother.

All about me

- **BORN:** 1910
- **DIED:** 1997
- **PLACE OF BIRTH:** Skopje, Macedonia
- **FACTOID:** My real name is Agnes Gonxha Bojaxhiu.
- **IN A NUTSHELL:** I heard stories about Christian missionaries as a child and decided to become one too and help people.

Mother Teresa

The CATHOLIC NUN who spent 45 years caring for the poor, sick, orphaned, and dying

The Missionaries

Teresa was horrified by the *poverty and suffering* she saw on the streets when she was teaching in **Kolkata**. She started a new order, called the Missionaries of Charity, who took in the sick and dying (including lepers) and cared for them. She also created many **ORPHANAGES**.

International recognition

Teresa's service to humanity drew worldwide recognition. She received **124 awards** for her charitable work and was given the **NOBEL PEACE PRIZE** in 1979. When she died, the Missionaries of Charity had 610 missions in 123 countries, which care for suffering people, and *feed and educate the poor*.

By the way...
I was beatified by Pope John Paul II in 2003, which is the first step to becoming a saint.

By 17, Teresa knew that she wanted to be a nun.

51

Sundarlal Bahuguna

The man who HUGGED trees and saved them from being cut

Sundarlal Bahuguna is a social activist who devoted his entire life to save the environment from commercial exploitation.

Early life

Sundarlal Bahuguna (b. 1927) was born in a village near **Tehri, Uttarakhand**. When he was 13, Bahuguna met Gandhian leader Dev Suman, who taught him about the *non-violent method of protest*. Inspired by the Mahatma, Bahuguna chose to live in a village, and dedicated all his time to save the Himalayan region from destruction.

Did you know?
Sundarlal Bahuguna was awarded the 1987 Right Livelihood Award for my work in the Chipko Movement.

Bahuguna drew global attention when he marched to the UN conference in Nairobi, Kenya, in 1985, with a bundle of firewood on his back.

The Chipko Movement

In the 1970s, forests in the Himalayan region were facing a threat from timber contractors. Village women of Uttarakhand formed a chain around the trees to save them from contractors' axes. Thus began the Chipko Movement (**Chipko means "to embrace"** in Hindi). In 1981, Bahuguna went on a *5,000-km (3,106-mile) march across the Himalayas*, gathering support for the movement. It ended in a meeting with then Prime Minister Indira Gandhi, who got an order passed to protect some parts of the Himalayan forests. This not only slowed down the deterioration of the region, but also made **DEFORESTATION A NATIONAL ISSUE.**

He couldn't have done it without...

MAHATMA GANDHI *(1869–1948) inspired Bahuguna to stand up against the ills of society* **WITHOUT RESORTING TO VIOLENCE.** *The Gandhian ways of protest are a part of his philosophy.*

Gandhi Peace Prize and Ramon Magsaysay Award winner **CHANDI PRASAD BHATT** *(b.1934) was one of the first* **CHIPKO ACTIVISTS** *to join hands with Bahuguna to save the environment.*

"Save the seeds"

The Beej Bachao Andolan, or "Save the Seeds" movement began in the late 1980s, when Bahuguna and a group of activists from the Tehri district, Uttarakhand, came up with the slogan, "Which gifts do forest bear: Soil, water, and fresh air". Mostly led by women, it also sought to preserve people's culture by fighting against government programmes that favoured the corporate sector.

By the way...
I also spearheaded the anti-alcohol drive from 1965 to 1970 by organizing hill women to spread awareness about the negative effects of alcohol.

Anti-Tehri Dam Movement

In the early 1990s, the government started constructing a dam on the Bhagirathi river, near Tehri in Uttarakhand, to generate electricity. Bahuguna feared that such a dam, once built, would completely drown Tehri and 40 other surrounding villages, and also cause a lot of damage to the environment. He went on a hunger strike to stop the construction and made the bank of the Bhagirathi his home during his 19-year-long battle against the dam. However, the government eventually had its way and the dam was built at the proposed site.

He paved the way for...

INSPIRED BY SUNDARLAL BAHUGUNA, MEDHA PATKAR *(b.1954) started the Narmada Bachao Andolan in 1989 to protest against the construction of dams on the Narmada river.*

All about me

- **BORN:** 1933
- **PLACE OF BIRTH:** Santiniketan, West Bengal
- **FACTOID:** I currently teach economics and philosophy at the Harvard University, USA.
- **IN A NUTSHELL:** In 2010, *Time* magazine included me in their list of "100 most influential persons in the world".

By the way... it was Rabindranath Tagore who gave me my name "Amartya", which means immortal.

Amartya Sen

A WELFARE ECONOMIST who thought of ways to help the poor

Food for thought

Amartya Sen was just a boy when he saw millions of **people die of starvation** during the Bengal famine of 1943. What struck him most was the fact that it was only **the poor who suffered**. After completing his education, he **taught economics** in India, the UK, and the USA. Before he started teaching, money and interest rate dominated the field of economics; Sen made **causes of POVERTY AND INEQUALITY** central to his research work.

Human Development Report

This annual report ranks countries on a variety of economic and social indicators such as health care, nutrition, jobs, and education.

Sen believes a food crisis is a result of a faulty and unequal distribution system.

Friend of the poor

Sen's views have **FORCED GOVERNMENTS** to **revise their economic policies** and to find ways to lessen the sufferings of the poor. His theories influenced the formulation of the **Human Development Report**, published every year by the *United Nations*. He won the **NOBEL PRIZE** in Economics in 1998 for his work on the **causes of famine**, and for coming up with *ways to avoid shortages of food*.

All about me

- **BORN:** 1946
- **PLACE OF BIRTH:** Chennai
- **FACTOID:** In the year 2000, I was presented with the Ramon Magsaysay Award for community leadership.
- **IN A NUTSHELL:** I helped pass the Right to Information Act, a major step in reducing the country's corruption.

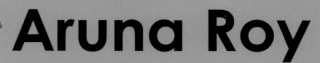

Aruna Roy

A SOCIAL ACTIVIST who made government records accessible to ordinary citizens

Since its inception, the MKSS has operated out of this house in Devdungri, Rajasthan.

Agent of change

Aruna Roy *gave up her career as an IAS officer* to become a **social activist**. Starting from a tiny village in the deserts of Rajasthan in the 1980s, Roy began a long campaign to fight for the rights of workers and peasants. She founded the Mazdoor Kisan Shakti Sangathan (MKSS) in 1987, an organization that **FIGHTS CORRUPTION** at the grassroots level.

A transparent system

Roy's landmark achievement was the **RIGHT TO INFORMATION (RTI) ACT**, a law that promoted the public's **right to access official records**. Adopted as a national law in 2005, the RTI Act has given country's poor a powerful tool to fight for their rights. It has **exposed** everything from land scams to bank thefts to the *misuse of funds* meant for the poor.

By the way... besides Tamil, Hindi, and English, I can speak in French as well.

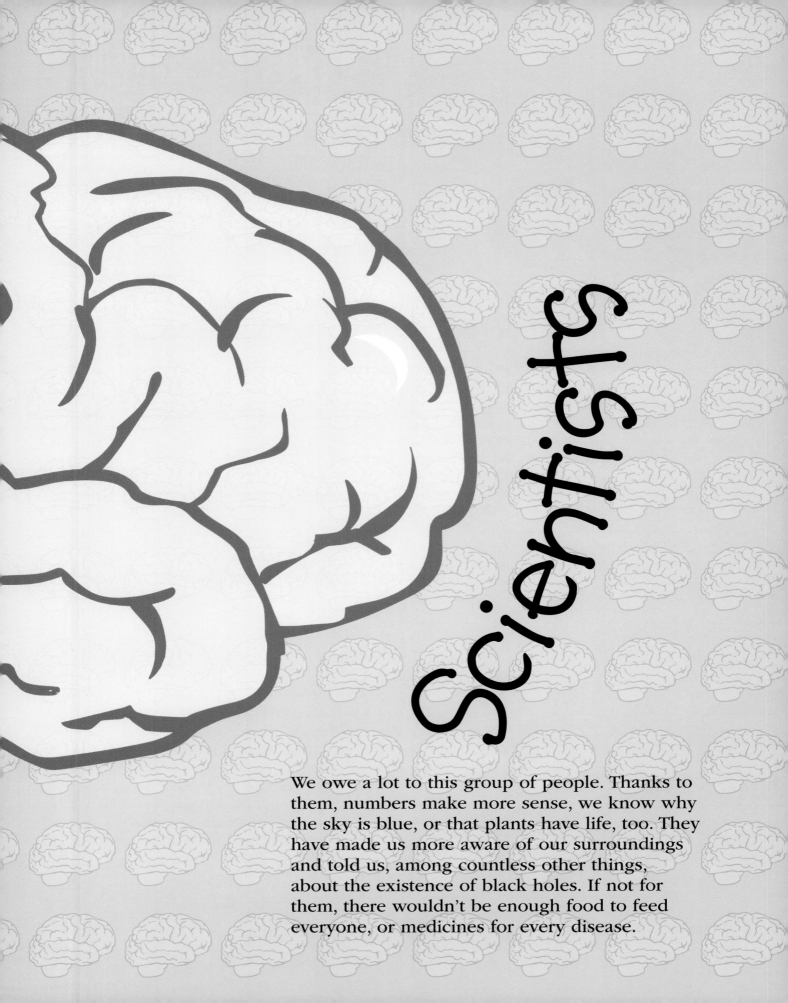

Scientists

We owe a lot to this group of people. Thanks to them, numbers make more sense, we know why the sky is blue, or that plants have life, too. They have made us more aware of our surroundings and told us, among countless other things, about the existence of black holes. If not for them, there wouldn't be enough food to feed everyone, or medicines for every disease.

Ancient pioneers

Many centuries ago, India was home to some of the greatest minds who made significant discoveries in the fields of science and astronomy, introducing ideas that the world had not known before.

EDUCATING the world

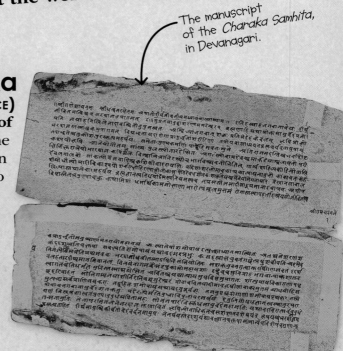

The manuscript of the *Charaka Samhita*, in Devanagari.

Acharya Charaka
(c. 300BCE)

Acharya Charaka was a noted **practitioner of the science of Ayurveda**, a system of medicine that originated in ancient India. Widely known as the "father of Indian medicine", he is said to have developed the basic principles of Ayurveda. *His principles, diagnoses, and cures hold true even today*, thousands of years later. His renowned work, the *Charaka Samhita*, is considered an **ENCYCLOPEDIA OF AYURVEDA**. He came up with cures for diseases such as diabetes, tuberculosis, and certain heart disorders. He also explained the importance of proper digestion and strong immunity.

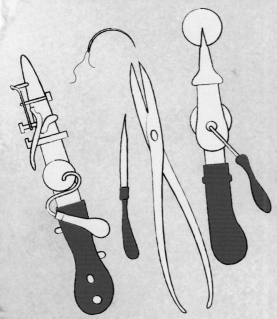

Sushruta
(c. 600BCE)

One of the **EARLIEST SURGEONS** known to the world, Sushruta lived and practised his art in present-day Varanasi. In his famous work, *Sushruta Samhita*, **he described over 120 surgical instruments and eight categories of surgical procedures**. He was the *first person to conduct a plastic surgery* – his technique of reconstructing noses is followed almost unchanged to this day. Because of his contribution to the art and science of surgery, he is often called the "**father of surgery**".

Sushruta described over 300 surgical procedures. ⇨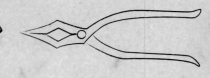

Aryabhatta
(c. 476–550BCE)

Aryabhatta was a **renowned mathematician and astronomer** of the classical age (the time period between 400 and 1200CE) of India. His contribution in mathematics is unparalleled – but he is best known for coming up with the **CONCEPT OF ZERO** (or *shunya*) in the numerical system. In the field of astronomy, Aryabhatta was the first to propose that the **Earth is spherical and it rotates on its own axis**, which results in day and night. He even concluded that the moon is dark and shines because of the light of the sun.

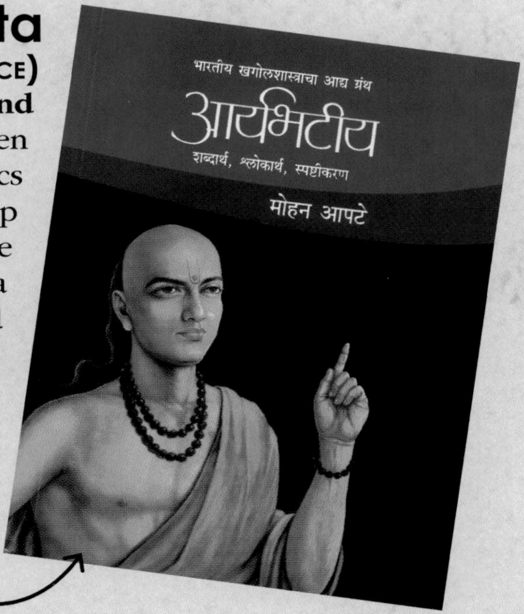

His best-known work, *Aryabhatiya*, covers many topics such as astronomy, trigonometry, arithmetic, and algebra.

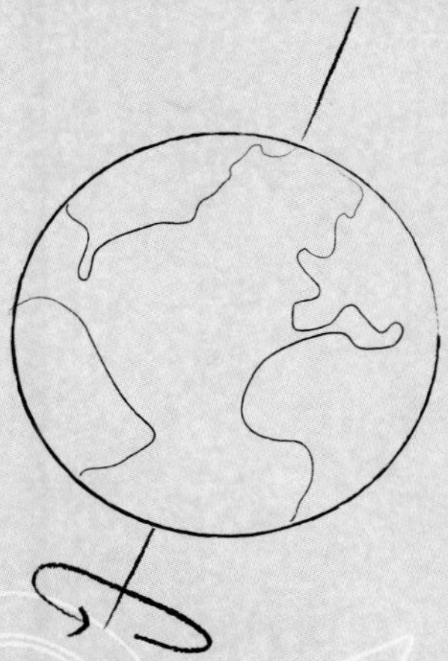

Aryabhatta was the one to infer that the Earth rotates on its axis daily.

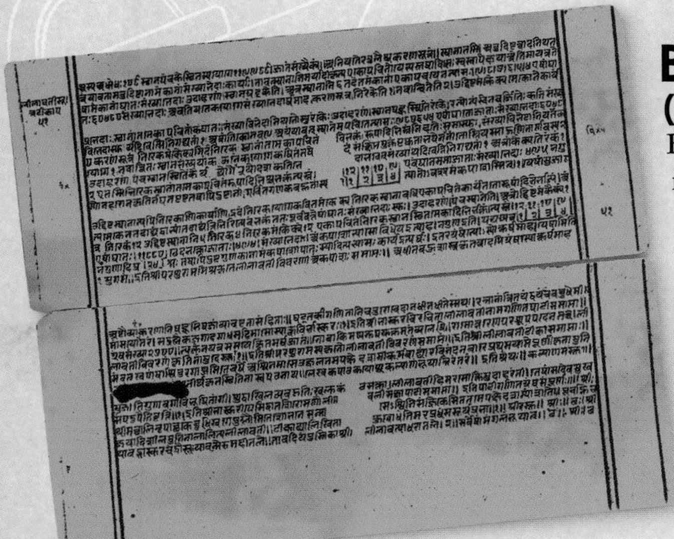

The manuscript of the *Siddhanta Shiromani*, in Devanagari.

Bhaskaracharya
(c. 1114–1185CE)

Bhaskaracharya was one of the most powerful minds of the 12th century. He was the **head of the astronomical observatory in Ujjain**, the leading mathematical centre of India in those times. He is said to have **DISCOVERED THE FORCE OF GRAVITY** 500 years before Isaac Newton did. He wrote two great books – the ***Siddhanta Shiromani*** on mathematics, and the ***Surya Siddhanta***, which talks about gravitational force and other astronomical quantities.

Bhaskaracharya explained eclipses as well.

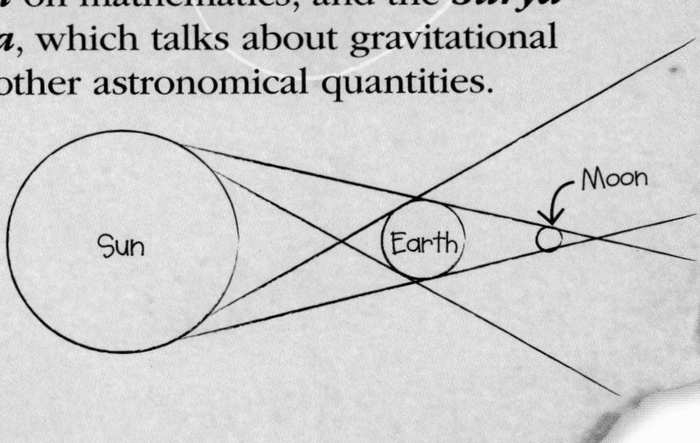

Sawai Jai Singh

The ASTRONOMER-KING of 18th-century India

The Maharaja of Jaipur was an astronomer and a town planner who founded the city of Jaipur and built some of the greatest astronomical wonders of India.

Did you know?
The Jantar Mantar in Jaipur has been declared a World Heritage Site by UNESCO, the international organization dedicated to preserving art and culture.

Reaching for the stars

Sawai Jai Singh (1688–1743), or Jai Singh II, was the ***ruler of Amber***, later called Jaipur. He showed a keen interest in **MATHEMATICS AND ASTRONOMY** from an early age. He became a king at the young age of 11, after the death of his father, Maharaja Bishan Singh, but his royal duties did not keep him away from pursuing his interests. Jai Singh followed some of the Islamic and European astronomers, such as **Ulugh Beg** and **La Hire**, and had their work ***translated into Sanskrit***.

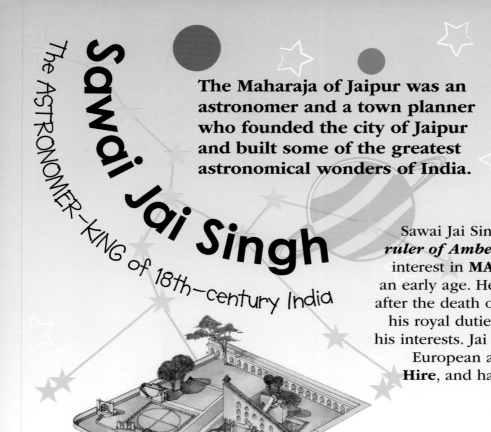

Of the five observatories, the Jaipur one is the most elaborate, and is located just outside the royal palace.

Damaged over time, the Jantar Mantar in Delhi was restored in 1901.

The Jantar Mantars

Jai Singh built five observatories, known as the Jantar Mantars, between 1724 and 1734. Literally meaning "***formula of instruments***" in Sanskrit, the Jantar Mantar was first built in **Delhi**, followed by **Jaipur**, **Mathura**, **Ujjain**, and **Varanasi**. All but the Mathura observatory still exist. Although Jai Singh borrowed some astronomical elements from Greek and Persian observatories, he built the Jantar Mantar on a much greater scale and in unique design, not seen before.

He couldn't have done it without...

Sawai Jai Singh followed the Uzbek astronomer **ULUGH BEG** *(1394–1449), and updated his famous work,* **CATALOGUE OF STARS**.

60

Named after Jai Singh, the Jaigarh Fort, also known as the Victory Fort, was built in 1726, to protect the Amber Fort, near Jaipur.

The Pink City

Jai Singh started the construction of Jaipur in 1727. **The first planned city of India**, it took four years to complete. It was designed by architect Vidyadhar Bhattacharya, based on *the principles of* **Shilpa Shastra**, *the ancient Indian text on architecture*. Divided into nine blocks or grids, the city had clearly demarcated areas for state buildings and palaces. In 1853, the whole city was painted pink to welcome the **PRINCE OF WALES**, on a royal visit to Jaipur. Some of the buildings still retain the colour.

By the way...
the Mughal Emperor Aurangzeb gave me the title *Sawai*, which implied that I was one and a quarter times superior to other kings of my time.

Astronomical instruments

Each of the Jantar Mantars consists of astronomical instruments, or *yantra*, made of stones and bricks, in various geometrical shapes and sizes. Samrat Yantra is a high-precision sundial that was used for measuring local time. Ram Yantra is a cylindrical structure used for predicting the altitude of celestial objects. Jai Prakash Yantra, made of two hollowed-out half-spheres, was used to map the position of the sun.

Jai Singh had Greek astronomer **PTOLEMY'S** *(100CE–170BCE) book* **ALMAGEST** *translated into Sanskrit to understand his work on astronomy.*

British astronomer **JOHN FLAMSTEED** *(1646–1719) listed the positions of 3000 stars. Jai Singh is said to have found* **AN ERROR OF HALF A DEGREE** *in the moon's position in Flamsteed's calculations.*

CV Raman

The FIRST ASIAN to receive a Nobel Prize in Physics

One of the greatest scientists of India, CV Raman is known the world over for his groundbreaking work in the field of physics.

A child genius

Chandrasekhara Venkata Raman (1888–1970) was born in the village of Tiruchirapalli, Tamil Nadu, to a physics lecturer and his wife. Raman **grew up in an atmosphere of science, music, and Sanskrit literature**. A *brilliant student* from the start, he was always curious to learn new things and understand various natural phenomena. He passed his Class 10 board exams at the age of 11, and **FINISHED HIS UNDERGRADUATE STUDIES WHEN HE WAS 15**.

Did you know?
Raman Effect paved the way for the science of modern optics. It is most commonly used in scanners that are used for security and medical checks.

When rays of light strike the surface of water, some of the rays scatter while passing through liquid, while some change in wavelength.

From accounts to science

In 1907, Raman began to work as an accountant **in Kolkata** after successfully clearing the Civil Services examination. Although this job occupied most of his time, Raman still managed to **SPARE HIS EVENINGS FOR SCIENTIFIC RESEARCH** at the laboratory of the Indian Association for the Cultivation of Science. On certain occasions, he would spend an entire night conducting experiments. Such was his passion for science that in 1917, he resigned from his job to become a *Professor of Physics at Calcutta University*.

He couldn't have done it without...

Raman was not convinced with English scientist **LORD RAYLEIGH'S** *(1842–1919) explanation that the sea was blue due to the colour of the sky, and thus went on to discover the Raman Effect.*

The Raman Effect

On a **sea voyage** to Europe in 1921, Raman **noticed the blue colour of the glaciers and the sea**. He wanted to find out where the blue colour came from. Once Raman returned to India, he performed many experiments to find an answer and ultimately established that when light passes through a transparent medium, some light beams change their wavelength while scattering. This discovery was called the **RAMAN EFFECT**, and fetched him the **NOBEL PRIZE** in Physics in 1930.

The Raman Effect explains why the sea appears blue. The colour blue has shorter wavelength, so it scatters more than other colours when light beams fall on water, and reaches our eyes faster.

He paved the way for...

The **RAMAN RESEARCH INSTITUTE** *was founded by Raman in 1948 to carry out further research. Located in Bengaluru, it is now a well-known research organization engaged in basic sciences.*

Raman was the founder and the first editor of the prestigious **INDIAN JOURNAL OF PHYSICS**, *published by the Indian Association for the Cultivation of Science since 1926.*

SN Bose

The man who first predicted the BOSON particle

All about me

- **BORN:** 1894
- **DIED:** 1974
- **PLACE OF BIRTH:** Kolkata, West Bengal
- **FACTOID:** Albert Einstein praised my breakthrough discovery in his biography *Subtle is the Lord*.
- **IN A NUTSHELL:** I gave the world the first clue about the existence of boson particles.

On reading Bose's letter, Einstein translated and published Bose's theory in a German magazine.

$E = h\nu$

Did you know? Bose's work with photons and their behaviour laid the foundation for the invention of the laser, a form of focused light – a beam of photons.

The Bose–Einstein connection

In a letter to celebrated **scientist Albert Einstein, in 1924**, Indian physicist Satyendra Nath Bose described how the particles of light, namely photons, behaved. Einstein was amazed by the contents of the letter. Bose's research helped Einstein to predict the existence of a **FIFTH STATE OF MATTER** – the Bose–Einstein Condensate, the other four being solid, liquid, gas, and plasma. This state forms when matter is super cooled and its particles have very low energy. *This condensate is made up of a dense collection of particles called "bosons", named after Bose.*

Built by CERN, the Hadron Collider is a huge atom–smashing machine that is trying to recreate the "Big Bang" – the phenomenon that explains the beginning of the universe.

The Higgs boson particle

In 1964, British physicist Peter Higgs predicted the existence of certain subatomic particles that had mass. The **Higgs boson particle, sometimes called the "God Particle"**, is a type of boson particle, explained more than 40 years ago by *SN Bose*. The Higgs boson was confirmed to exist in 2012 by scientists running the **LARGE HADRON COLLIDER**, a complex scientific machine, located at the European Organization for Nuclear Research (CERN) in Switzerland. This discovery will bring scientists closer to understanding the composition of all matter.

All about me

- **BORN:** 1858
- **DIED:** 1937
- **PLACE OF BIRTH:** Bikrampur (now in Bangladesh)
- **FACTOID:** I studied in a Bengali-medium school and learned English much later in Kolkata.
- **IN A NUTSHELL:** I was a physicist and botanist, with a keen interest in literature.

JC Bose

The scientist who proved to the world that PLANTS HAVE LIFE

The true inventor

Dr Jagdish Chandra Bose was one of those remarkable scientists who made great discoveries in two different scientific fields – physics and botany. In 1895, Bose demonstrated the **USE OF RADIO WAVES** and showed that **communication signals can be sent without using wires.** However, Bose *did not patent the apparatus that helped him detect radio waves.* Guglielmo Marconi, the Italian scientist, is generally recognized as the inventor of the wireless radio.

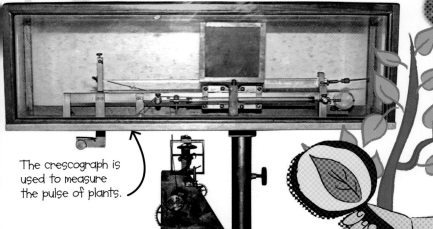

The crescograph is used to measure the pulse of plants.

Giving life to plants

Another wonderful discovery of Bose was in connection with plant life. He proved that **PLANTS HAVE LIFE, TOO** – they are sensitive to heat, cold, light, noise, and other external factors. He **invented an instrument called the crescograph,** which could *record the response of plants* under different conditions, showing that there are many similarities between plants and other living beings.

Did you know?
A great lover of literature, Bose also found time to write science fiction in Bengali – between his experiments.

S Ramanujan

The man who loved NUMBERS

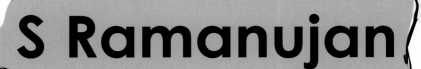

All about me

- **BORN:** 1887
- **DIED:** 1920
- **PLACE OF BIRTH:** Erode, Tamil Nadu
- **FACTOID:** I proposed 3,900 formulae. A lot of them have been proved right and are used in mathematical calculations.
- **IN A NUTSHELL:** I am a mathematician who made significant contributions to fields such as mathematical analysis and number theory.

Letter to Hardy

In 1913, the English mathematician GH Hardy (1877–1947) received a 10-page letter from an unknown clerk in Chennai. The letter contained *120 mathematical theorems*, which Hardy initially did not pay attention to. But something about the formulae made him look a second time and he realized that the **mathematical results were a work of genius**. He immediately arranged for Srinivasa Ramanujan, the writer of the letter, to come to England, and thus began a very successful **HARDY–RAMANUJAN COLLABORATION**.

Ramanujan spent five years in Cambridge, England, between 1914 and 1919, during which he worked very closely with GH Hardy.

Did you know?

During the last year of his life Ramanujan wrote most of his mathematical discoveries on loose sheafs of paper, which were later discovered by mathematician George Andrews, who gave it the name "The Lost Notebook".

The English term

Ramanujan's stay in England was quite productive. He wrote papers on topics such as the *infinite series* and *number theory* – an abstract study of the structure of number systems. **Cambridge granted him a Bachelor of Science degree** in 1916. He was also **ELECTED A FELLOW OF THE ROYAL SOCIETY** – only the second Indian to get such an honour.

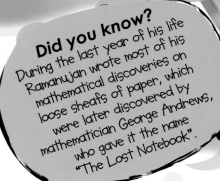

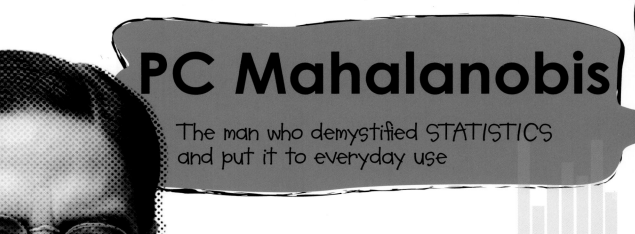

PC Mahalanobis

The man who demystified STATISTICS and put it to everyday use

All about me

- **BORN:** 1893
- **DIED:** 1972
- **PLACE OF BIRTH:** Kolkata, West Bengal
- **FACTOID:** The Indian Statistical Institute started as a statistical laboratory from my room in Presidency College, Kolkata.
- **IN A NUTSHELL:** I was responsible for nearly all statistical work done in India between the 1920s and mid-1930s.

Numbers tell a story

A chance reading of the statistical journal *Biometrika* at the University of Cambridge, England, left Prasanta Chandra Mahalanobis totally smitten by the subject. He used statistics to study a vast range of topics – from analysing the cultural differences of Anglo-Indians in Kolkata to trying to understand the tea-drinking habit of the middle class in the city. In 1936, he conceptualized the "*Mahalanobis Distance*", a statistical measure to study and compare an unknown data set to a known one.

By the way...
I was awarded the Weldon Medal by the Oxford University in 1944, and the Indian government gave me the Padma Vibhushan in 1968 for my contributions to statistics.

Mahalanobis started the statistical journal *Sankhya*, which literally means "numbers".

Nation building

A visionary, Mahalanobis founded the **Indian Statistical Institute** in 1931 to develop statistics as a discipline. He realized the significance of statistics in national planning and established the **National Sample Survey Organization** for conducting regular socio-economic surveys. As a member of the **PLANNING COMMISSION**, he recommended rapid industrialization of India in its second Five Year Plan.

The Indian Statistical Institute, Kolkata

Homi J Bhabha

FATHER of the Indian nuclear energy programme

A creative scientist, Homi Bhabha helped India develop world-class nuclear capabilities.

By the way... as a child, I could barely sleep – a fact that constantly troubled my parents. They thought something was wrong with me until a doctor assured them that I was fine, just a little hyperactive.

Bhabha envisaged the vast potential of nuclear energy in the field of power generation.

He couldn't have done it without...

Prime Minister **JAWAHARLAL NEHRU** *(1889–1964) shared an excellent rapport with Bhabha and* **SUPPORTED HIS VISION** *of the use of nuclear energy for peaceful purposes.*

Bright son of India

Homi Jehangir Bhabha (1909–1966) was born in a wealthy Parsi family in Mumbai. A brilliant student, **he went to Cambridge University**, England, for an undergraduate course in mechanical engineering. Bhabha, however, had set his heart on another subject, so after finishing his engineering degree, he stayed back in Cambridge to do a doctorate in physics. As a *fellow of the Royal Society*, London, Bhabha got a chance to rub shoulders with some of the **GREATEST SCIENTISTS** of the time.

After obtaining his PhD in 1934, Bhabha stayed on in Cambridge to do research in physics.

A visionary

Bhabha was on a vacation in India in 1939, when the Second World War broke out. Unable to go back to Cambridge, **Bhabha joined the Indian Institute of Science, Bengaluru**, then headed by CV Raman, as a Reader in physics. Keen to set up a nuclear research centre, he wrote to JRD Tata, a close family friend, for support. Subsequently, the *Tata Institute for Fundamental Research* was formed in 1945, and under Bhabha's leadership became a major centre of **COSMIC RAY RESEARCH**.

A painter-scientist

Homi Bhabha was not just a great scientist – he also took keen interest in art and literature. In fact, he spent all his free time making sketches and painting. According to Bhabha, "art made life worth living". Many of his paintings are on display at the Tata Institute for Fundamental Research (TIFR).

Atoms for peace

Bhabha was of the firm belief that nuclear energy should be used for **CONSTRUCTIVE PURPOSES** and opposed the making of an atom bomb. He was instrumental in setting up the *Atomic Energy Commission of India, in 1948*, to promote nuclear research in the country. Under his guidance, Asia's first atomic reactor became operational at Trombay, in 1956.

In 1956, Bhabha sealed the deal with the USA to buy heavy water fuel for the peaceful use of atomic energy.

He paved the way for...

Bhabha helped set up the **ATOMIC ENERGY ESTABLISHMENT** in 1954, in Mumbai, which was later renamed after him as the **BHABHA ATOMIC RESEARCH CENTRE (BARC)**.

Bhabha visualized an atomic programme that would utilize **THORIUM AS A FUEL**. Today, it is seen as one of the **MOST PROMISING SOURCES OF NUCLEAR ENERGY**.

Subrahmanyan Chandrasekhar

The Indian–American scientist who explained the evolution of massive stars to the world.

The man who hinted at the existence of BLACK HOLES

Early life in India

Subrahmanyan Chandrasekhar (1910–1995) was born in Lahore, in present-day Pakistan, where his father was posted as an accountant-general. ***Tutored at home until the age of 12***, Chandrasekhar later shifted to Chennai and completed his school education from the Hindu High School. Inspired by his uncle, **CV Raman**, the Nobel Prize winner in Physics, to study science, Chandrasekhar joined the Presidency College, Chennai, for a bachelor's in physics. In 1930, he went to **CAMBRIDGE, ENGLAND, TO PURSUE HIGHER STUDIES**.

Star collapses after using its fuel to become a white dwarf.

A white dwarf will fade over time to become a black dwarf.

Sun–like star

Red giant

Star more massive than the sun

Supernova

Black holes are objects so dense that even light cannot escape.

Exploding and collapsing stars

At Cambridge, Chandrasekhar studied the structure of white dwarf stars. Stars, such as the sun, first expand to form red giants, but when they use up all their fuel, ***these sun-like stars collapse to form white dwarfs***. In 1932, he calculated that white dwarfs **1.4 times more massive than the sun** would continue to collapse until they **TURN INTO A BLACK HOLE**. The upper limit that he set for the mass of a white dwarf later came to be known as the Chandrasekhar Limit.

He couldn't have done it without...

*Chandrasekhar described his meeting with German physicist **Arnold Sommerfeld** (1868–1951) in 1928 as the most inspiring incident of his career.*

Late recognition

Chandrasekhar was not even 20 years old when he made his calculation for the Chandrasekhar Limit. When he first proposed the concept, not many scientists, including **physicists Arthur Eddington and Albert Einstein**, were ready to accept his findings. The much-awaited recognition came nearly *50 years later, in 1983*, when he was awarded (along with the nuclear astrophysicist WA Fowler) the **NOBEL PRIZE** in Physics for explaining the structure and evolution of massive stars.

By the way...
in 1937, I joined the University of Chicago, USA, as a Research Associate. Later, in 1953, I became a US citizen, and remained in the country for the rest of my life.

Black holes
While physicists such as Arthur Eddington, Albert Einstein, and Chandrasekhar explained the concept behind black holes, it was the American scientist John Wheeler who first coined the term "black hole" in 1967.

He paved the way for...

In 1999, NASA launched an X-ray observatory, called the **CHANDRA OBSERVATORY**, in Florida, USA, to acknowledge Chandrasekhar's contribution in the field of astrophysics.

The world's highest observatory, the **INDIAN ASTRONOMICAL OBSERVATORY** in Ladakh, houses a telescope named "Chandra" in honour of the stellar scientist.

71

Vikram Sarabhai

FATHER of the Indian space programme

All about me

- **BORN:** 1919
- **DIED:** 1971
- **PLACE OF BIRTH:** Ahmedabad, Gujarat
- **FACTOID:** I was instrumental in setting up the Indian Institute of Management (IIM) in Ahmedabad in 1961.
- **IN A NUTSHELL:** I wanted to use my knowledge of science to improve the condition of the common people.

Man with a vision

Vikram Sarabhai believed that science in general and space technology in particular could **take India on the path of development**. In 1947, after completing his PhD from the University of Cambridge, England, he came back to India and set up the ***Physical Research Laboratory (PRL)***, in Ahmedabad, with support from his parents. This was India's first research centre, which later expanded to become the **HEADQUARTERS FOR ALL SPACE ACTIVITIES**.

By the way...

I negotiated with National Aeronautics and Space Administration (NASA) to start the Satellite Instructional Television Experiment, which made educational TV shows for rural India.

Rohini-75 SSTC was the first rocket to be launched from TERLS, the launch pad in Kerala. TERLS was later renamed after Vikram Sarabhai.

St Mary Magdalene's Church served as the main office for the TERLS scientists.

The Indian space programme

Sarabhai set up the **Thumba Equatorial Rocket Launching Station (TERLS)** in 1962, with support from another eminent scientist, Homi Bhabha. Convinced of the immense possibilities of space technology in the field of education and communication, he established the ***Indian Space Research Organization (ISRO)*** in 1969. He helped build the **FIRST INDIAN SATELLITE, ARYABHATTA I**, which was sent into space in 1975, four years after Sarabhai's death.

All about me

- **BORN:** 1949
- **PLACE OF BIRTH:** Patiala, Punjab
- **FACTOID:** I was given the "Hero of the Soviet Union" award by the erstwhile USSR.
- **IN A NUTSHELL:** While in space, I experimented with "zero gravity yoga" to fight space sickness.

Rakesh Sharma

The FIRST INDIAN in space

Aboard space station Salyut 7, Sharma and his team conducted several biomedical experiments.

By the way...
in 1985, the government of India presented me with the Ashoka Chakra, the highest peacetime gallantry award for an individual.

Wings of desire

Rakesh Sharma joined the **Indian Air Force** as a pilot in 1970. A bright officer, Sharma is known to have flown 21 combat missions during the Indo-Pak war of 1971. Having proved his credibility, he swiftly rose through the ranks, and in 1984, became a *Squadron Leader* in the Indian Air Force.

Indo-Soviet space mission

Rakesh Sharma was selected from hundreds of applicants to become a cosmonaut for the Indo-Soviet joint space programme. In 1984, he became the first Indian to go into space, spending nearly eight days in the *Salyut 7* space station. While he was in space, then Prime Minister Indira Gandhi asked Sharma, over a voice channel, how India looked from space. The cosmonaut replied, "**SAARE JAHAN SE ACHCHA**", or "better than the whole world".

All about me

- **BORN:** 1925
- **PLACE OF BIRTH:** Kumbakonam, Tamil Nadu
- **FACTOID:** *Time* magazine has hailed me as one of the 20 most influential Asians of the 20th century.
- **IN A NUTSHELL:** I used my research skills in genetic engineering to help rid the world of hunger and poverty.

India grew 94 million tonnes of wheat in 2013, as compared to 12 million tonnes in the early 1960s.

By the way... I am the first person to win the World Food Prize, in 1987, for spearheading the introduction of high-yielding crop varieties in India.

Green Revolution

In the 1950s, *famines were a recurring phenomenon in India*. To solve this problem, Mankombu Sambasivan Swaminathan decided to introduce a **MEXICAN** semi-dwarf wheat variety, which produced three times more grain than other varieties in India. Steeped in traditional ways of agriculture, Indian farmers had to be convinced to use these seeds. MS set up 2,000 model farms to show them the benefits of these seeds.

Importer turns exporter

Swaminathan transformed India from an importer to *exporter of foodgrains*, increasing the total yield of wheat from 12 million tonnes to **23 MILLION TONNES,** ending India's reliance on imports. He worked on policies that helped India gain **long-term food sufficiency.**

MS Swaminathan

The agricultural scientist who led the GREEN REVOLUTION in India

All about me

- **BORN:** 1896
- **DIED:** 1987
- **PLACE OF BIRTH:** Mumbai, Maharashtra
- **FACTOID:** The long years I spent in the field studying birds made me one of those rare Indians who knew every part of the country.
- **IN A NUTSHELL:** I always liked to study birds in their natural environment.

Salim Ali
The BIRDMAN of India

As part of his survey in the princely state of Hyderabad, Salim Ali studied the Indian Roller bird, found across tropical Asia.

Man with a plan

Salim Ali struggled with years of **UNEMPLOYMENT** during the early phase of his life. Things turned around when he offered to *carry out a survey of avian life* in the princely states of India, such as Hyderabad, for free. The rulers of these states jumped at the idea of having their avian wildlife catalogued. Thus began Ali's career as a **field ornithologist**.

By the way...
I visited the Bombay Natural History Museum – the largest centre of bird research in India – as a child, which triggered my fascination with birds.

Ali's survey notes became the basis for the *Book of Indian Birds*.

In company of birds

It was assumed that the bird **FINN'S BAYA** had gone extinct more than 100 years ago, but Salim Ali **rediscovered** the species in the mountain ranges of Kumaon. He shared many such exraordinary findings in his books such as the ***Book of Indian Birds***, which sparked an interest in the birds of India among bird lovers. Ali also co-authored the ***Handbook of the Birds of India and Pakistan***.

Hargobind Khorana

The biochemist who cracked the GENETIC CODE

All about me

- **BORN:** 1922
- **DIED:** 2011
- **PLACE OF BIRTH:** Raipur, Punjab (now in Pakistan)
- **FACTOID:** I came from a poor family but gained a scholarship to study at Cambridge, where I developed an interest in nucleic acids and proteins.

IN A NUTSHELL: I helped to understand how the genetic code in a cell is used to make proteins.

Cracking the code

DNA, or deoxyribonucleic acid, is the set of instructions that lives in the cells of every creature. It is made up of **FOUR CHEMICAL BASES** called nucleotides – adenine, guanine, cytosine, thymine – in a certain order. **It is this order that determines the DNA's instructions**. Scientists tried to understand how these instructions were used to join amino acids, in a specific order, for the **manufacture of proteins** – chemicals that regulate the functions of life.

By the way...
I was the first to synthesize oligonucleotides (strings of nucleotides). Today, these are important tools in biotechnology, widely used in biology labs for cloning and genetic engineering.

Protein folds up into a shape determined by its sequence of amino acids.

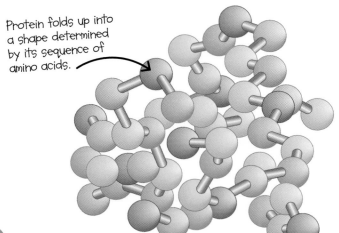

A Nobel breakthrough

At the University of Wisconsin, USA, Dr Hargobind Khorana, and some other scientists working independently, showed that **DNA nucleotides form a three-letter word** that specifies which amino acids are to be joined to proteins. It is how these three nucleotides work – the "words" in the code – that his colleagues tried to understand. Khorana confirmed the belief that each code is transmitted by separate and distinct three-letter "words" and **found the precise order of the nucleotides** within each triplet. In 1968, Khorana was awarded the **NOBEL PRIZE** in Medicine along with two other scientists.

All about me

- **BORN:** 1952
- **PLACE OF BIRTH:** Chidambaram, Tamil Nadu
- **FACTOID:** After completing my research training, I applied to 50 universities in the USA for a faculty position but didn't get a single job offer.
- **IN A NUTSHELL:** I started my career as a physicist, but ended up as a successful biologist.

By the way… I like cycling and trekking. I don't own a car, and I cycle to work.

From physics to biology

Venkataraman Ramakrishnan was born to scientist parents. His father wanted him to **become a doctor**. But young Venkataraman had other plans – instead he enrolled himself for an undergraduate course in physics in a college in Vadodara, Gujarat. He went to the USA for higher studies and **STARTED HIS CAREER AS A PHYSICIST**. However, his interest shifted to biology, when he read an article in the **Scientific American** about techniques to understand the structure of ribosomes – **the tiny units found within all living cells – that manufacture protein**.

Understanding the ribosome's structure helps pharmaceutical companies to develop new medicines to fight the growing problem of drug resistance in the human body.

The mystery of ribosomes

Between 2000 and 2002, Venkataraman, along with two other scientists, worked out the **exact structure and functions of a key part of ribosomes** (30S) and how it makes proteins – the building blocks of all living beings. This was a major breakthrough and in 2009, he was awarded the **NOBEL PRIZE** in Chemistry, which he shared with his fellow researchers.

Venkataraman Ramakrishnan

The man who unlocked the key to RIBOSOMES

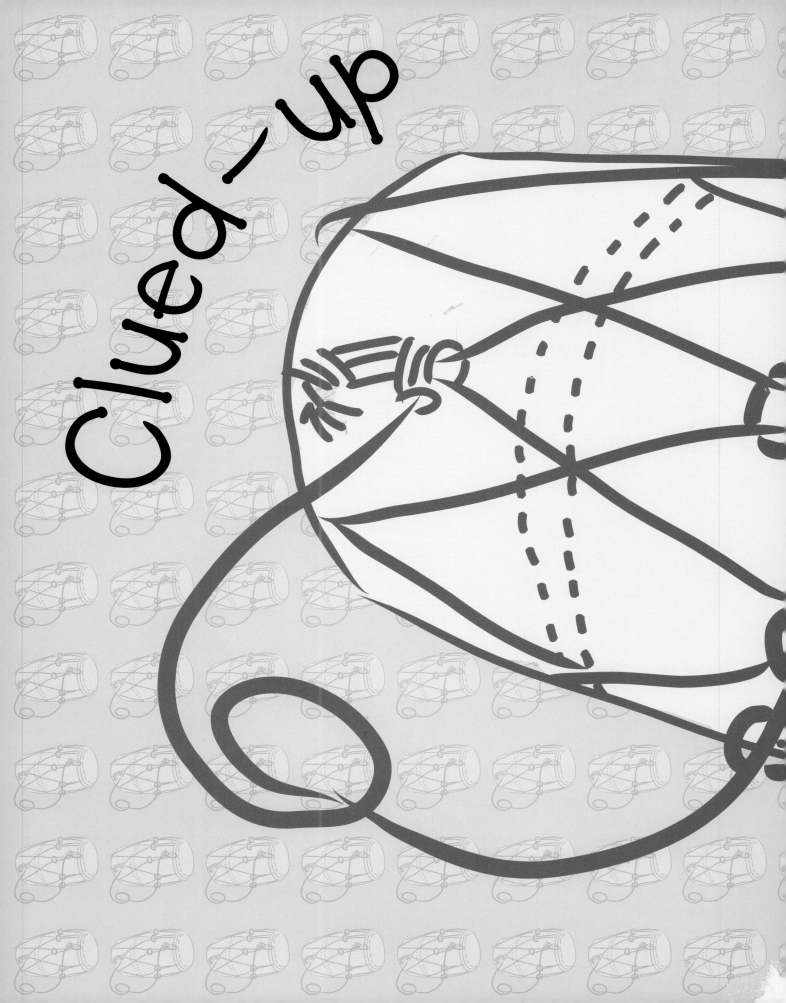

Clued-up

Creatives

The world just wouldn't be the same without these rare talents who have brightened our lives with their creations. They have entertained us with their stories, poems, art, paintings, music, and movies. Thanks to them, boredom isn't an option.

Kalidasa

The man who is known as the GREATEST Sanskrit poet and dramatist

Did you know?
Meghaduta ("Cloud Messenger") is a love poem about a man waiting for his beloved on top of a mountain. It has lyrical descriptions of the mountains, rivers, and forests of north India.

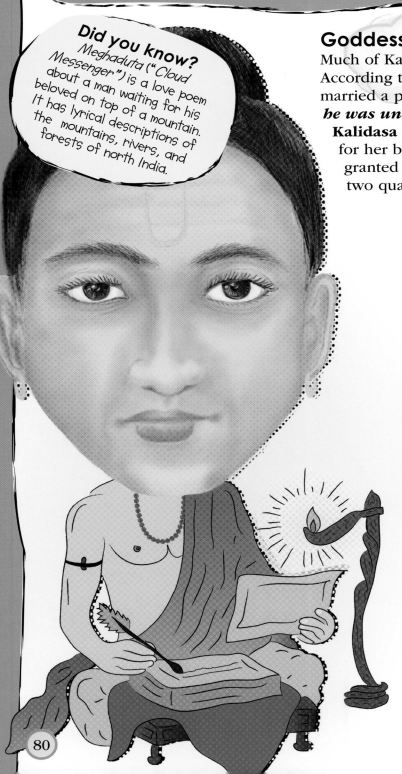

Goddess Kali's gift

Much of Kalidasa's personal life is the stuff of folklore. According to an unconfirmed account, Kalidasa married a princess, but *when she discovered that he was uneducated, she left him*. Humiliated, **Kalidasa prayed to goddess Kali**, asking her for her blessings. Goddess Kali is said to have granted him **WISDOM AND INTELLECT**, the two qualities Kalidasa is known for.

Considered a masterpiece, *Abhijananasakuntalam* tells the love story of King Dushyanta and Shakuntala, daughter of a sage.

Poems and dramas

We know about Kalidasa mostly by the great works he left behind. They reveal his mastery over the Sanskrit language and understanding of natural phenomena. He wrote three dramas, two epics, and two poems. *Abhijanasakuntalam* ("The Remembrance of Shakuntala") and *Malavikagnimitra* ("Malavika and Agnimitra") are two of his well-known plays. His lyrical poem *Meghaduta* ("Cloud Messenger") describes the city of Ujjain in central India in beautiful verses, hinting at his personal association with it.

All about me

■ **BORN:** 1767
■ **DIED:** 1847
■ **PLACE OF BIRTH:** Tiruvarur, Tamil Nadu
■ **FACTOID:** I sang around 24,000 songs, out of which only 700 exist today.
■ **IN A NUTSHELL:** I was one of the greatest classical composers, who sang to connect with God.

A bronze statue of St Thyagaraja, who was revered as a master musician

Mystical musings

Thyagaraja **began learning music at an early age**, under an eminent music scholar Sonti Venkataramaiah. A devotee of Lord Rama, Thyagaraja saw music as a way to reach God. He was only 13 when he composed "Namo Namo Raghavayya", a song in praise of Lord Rama. Impressed by Thyagaraja's compositions, the ***King of Thanjavur invited him to his court to honour him***. Thyagaraja, however, declined the invitation, preferring to **REMAIN A DEVOTEE OF RAMA** than sing for the King.

Did you know?
A crater on the planet Mercury, located near its equator, has been named after Thyagaraja.

Thyagaraja played the veena, a long-necked lute, popularly used in Carnatic music.

Classical legacy

Thyagaraja is credited with **laying down the foundation of south Indian classical (Carnatic) music**. He composed thousands of devotional songs, most of them in Telugu. His **PANCHARATNA KRITIS** ("Five Gems") is a set of five songs that remains to this day one of the best compositions of Carnatic music, and is sung even now at every classical musical event.

Thyagaraja
The SAINT-MUSICIAN whose devotional melodies live on

Rabindranath Tagore

The first NOBEL LAUREATE of India

By the way...
I am the only poet whose works have been chosen to be the national anthems of two countries: India and Bangladesh.

Rabindranath Tagore loved literature, painting, and music. He introduced Indian culture to the West through his beautiful creations.

Early life

Tagore was born in a wealthy family in Bengal, in 1861. He was mostly **TUTORED AT HOME** in Kolkata, as he found school boring and restricting. He briefly *studied law* in London, but soon lost interest and **came back to India without a degree**.

Poet, painter, writer

From a young age, Tagore was interested in literature. He was **eight** when he wrote his **FIRST POEM**. He also wrote musical dramas, two autobiographies, and travel diaries. Among his 50 volumes of poetry are *Sonar Tari* (The Golden Boat, 1894) and *Gitimalya* (The Wreath of Songs, 1914).

Tagore's painting *Woman's face* featured on a 1978 Indian postage stamp.

He couldn't have done it without...

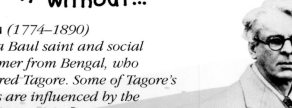

LALON *(1774–1890) was a Baul saint and social reformer from Bengal, who inspired Tagore. Some of Tagore's songs are influenced by the simplicity of the* **BAUL WAY OF LIFE**.

WILLIAM BUTLER YEATS *(1865–1939) was an Irish poet who helped publish Tagore's poems. Yeats also wrote the introduction to* GITANJALI.

Santiniketan

Tagore believed that the best learning happens when people live in **harmony with nature**. With this thought in mind, he started **SANTINIKETAN** under a tree, with only five students. The school is located near Bolpur, West Bengal, and later expanded into a central university – **Visva-Bharati** – in 1951. Indira Gandhi, Satyajit Ray, and Amartya Sen were some of its illustrious students.

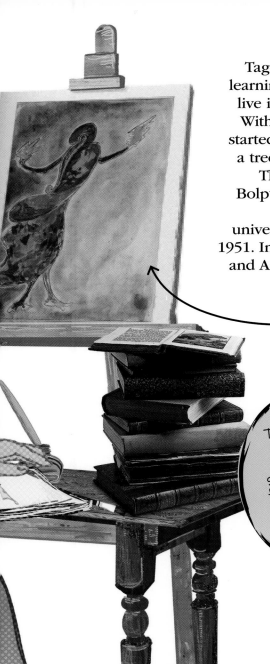

Tagore's famous painting *Dancing woman* was made with ink on paper.

> ### Did you know?
> Tagore was knighted in 1915 for his contribution to literature. He, however, surrendered the title in 1919 following the Jallianwala Bagh massacre, when the British troops killed several innocent Indians.

Rabindra Sangeet

Tagore also **loved music**, and wrote and composed more than **2,000 songs**. These compositions are known as **"RABINDRA SANGEET"**, and are still popular. These songs are a fusion of folk, Hindustani, and Western classical music, with a distinct style of their own. Musician Pankaj Mallick (1902–1974) and singer Hemant Kumar (1920–1989) were inspired by these songs.

A song offering

In 1913, Tagore became the first Asian to win the Nobel Prize in Literature for *Gitanjali* (*Song Offerings*). A collection of poems, *Gitanjali* was written by Tagore to express his devotion to God.

He paved the way for...

Famous Chilean poet and Nobel prize-winner **PABLO NERUDA** *(1904–1973) has written poems on* **NATURE** *in the same style as* **TAGORE'S**.

Publisher of the literary magazine **SUR**, **VICTORIA OCAMPO** *(1890–1979) greatly admired Tagore. The Argentinean was an inspiration for many of his poems such as* **PURABI**.

Writers on the block

The magic of STORYTELLING

Premchand's works have been translated into English and Russian.

Munshi Premchand
(1880–1936)

A writer of **Hindi and Urdu fiction**, Premchand's real name was **Dhanpat Rai**. He wrote nearly 300 stories and novels. Some of his works have been made into films, such as *Godaan* and *Karmabhoomi*. His writings were *not mere entertainment*, as he used them to convey **SOCIAL MESSAGES** and criticize social ills and evils. A master of stories, some of his best works include short stories, such as **Idgah, Shatranj ke Khiladi, and Lottery.**

Amrita Pritam
(1919–2005)

Punjabi literature could not boast of any prominent **woman author** until Amrita Pritam came to the fore. *Starting as a romantic poet*, she soon shifted attention to **SOCIAL ISSUES** at hand. She is best known for her writings on women, dreams, and her experiences during the *partition of India*. Her most notable novel *Pinjar* was adapted into a film in 2003.

For centuries, authors have been among the world's most important people, helping record history and keeping us entertained. Whether in fiction, prose, or poetry, these Indian authors have kept that tradition alive.

Vikram Seth
(b. 1952)

Seth was born in Kolkata, studied in England and the USA, and lived for some time in China to research Chinese poetry. He combines elements from these **four vastly different cultures in his writings**, based on his experiences and travels. Seth has studied many languages and is a ***storehouse of knowledge*** on a huge variety of subjects, including philosophy, politics, and economics. **He plays** the **FLUTE** and the **CELLO**, and sings the German "lieder" (romantic poems). Among his most popular works are ***The Golden Gate*** and ***A Suitable Boy***.

Amitav Ghosh
(b.1956)

A novelist, travel writer, and journalist, Amitav Ghosh is **known** not only in India, but ***all over the world***. He has won many awards, such as the Sahitya Akademi Award for ***The Shadow Lines*** and the Arthur C Clarke Award for ***The Calcutta Chromosome***. In 2008, his book ***The Sea of Poppies*** was nominated for the Man Booker Prize. His work has been translated into more than **20 LANGUAGES**. He has a unique style of storytelling, **blending fact with fiction**, creating unusual characters, and sometimes even new languages!

Amitav Ghosh grew up in India, Bangladesh, and Sri Lanka.

Dadasaheb Phalke

The FATHER of Indian cinema

At a time when nobody had heard about films or filmmaking, Dadasaheb Phalke studied the art and pioneered filmmaking in India.

The narrative begins…

Dadasaheb Phalke was born in 1870 in Trimbakeshwar, Maharashtra. *Creatively inclined* from a young age, Dadasaheb studied at the Sir JJ School of Arts in Mumbai and the Kala Bhavan in Vadodra, where he learned **drawing, painting, and photography**. Although he started with the printing business, he was to soon find **HIS REAL CALLING**.

A "filmi" twist of fate

Around 1910, Dadasaheb chanced upon the silent film *The Life of Christ*. After watching the film, he began to wonder if such **movies could be made in India** with Indian themes. What began as an idle curiosity soon turned into an obsession, motivating him to raise money and *experiment with a few short films*.

He paved the way for...

Dadasaheb was a visionary who laid the foundation for the INDIAN FILM INDUSTRY in an age when cinema had no place in a common man's life.

One of the most coveted honours of Indian cinema, the **DADASAHEB PHALKE AWARD** is given to great achievers in recognition of their lifetime contributions to Indian cinema.

Did you know?
At a time when acting was taboo for women, Dadasaheb introduced a female actor in a lead role in his film *Mohini Bhasmasur* (1913).

Fitting tribute
In 2009, Paresh Mokashi, a theatre veteran, made a Marathi film called *Harishchandrachi Factory*, which captures Dadasaheb's struggles during the making of his first feature film, *Raja Harishchandra*.

Where it began
Dadasaheb embarked on his celluloid journey in 1913 with ***Raja Harishchandra*, India's first full-length motion picture.** He had to borrow money from his wife to make this film, which became an instant success. Dadasaheb went on to make many more movies.

Some of his most noted works include *Satyavan Savitri* (1914), *Lanka Dahan* (1917), and *Kaliya Mardan* (1919).

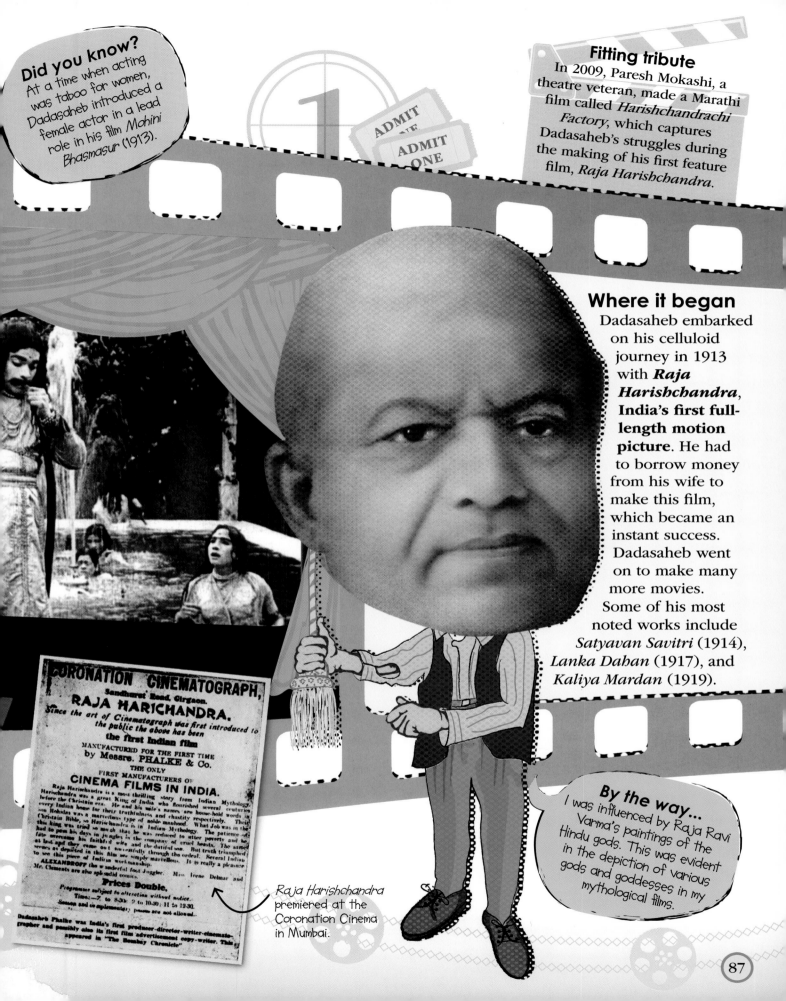

CORONATION CINEMATOGRAPH,
Sandhurst Road, Girgaon.
RAJA HARICHANDRA.
Since the art of Cinematograph was first introduced to the public the above has been
the first Indian film
MANUFACTURED FOR THE FIRST TIME
by Messrs. PHALKE & Co.
THE ONLY
FIRST MANUFACTURERS OF
CINEMA FILMS IN INDIA.

Raja Harischandra is a most thrilling story from Indian Mythology. Harischandra was a great King of India who flourished several centuries before the Christian era. He and his wife's names are household words in every Indian home for their truthfulness and chastity respectively. Their son Rohidas was a marvellous type of noble manhood. What Job was in the Christian Bible, so Harischandra is in Indian Mythology. The patience of this king was tried so much that he was reduced to utter poverty and he had to pass his days in the jungles in the company of cruel beasts. The same late overcame his faithful wife and the dutiful son. But truth triumphed at last and they came out successfully through the ordeal. Several Indian scenes as depicted in this film are simply marvellous. It is really a pleasure to see this piece of Indian workmanship.

ALEXANDROFF the wonderful foot Juggler. Miss Irene Delmar and Mr. Clements are also splendid comics.

Prices Double.

Programme subject to alteration without notice.
Time:—7, to 8.30; 9 to 10.30; 11 to 12.30.
Season and supplementary passes are not allowed.

Dadasaheb Phalke was India's first producer-director-writer-cinematographer and possibly also its first film advertisement copy-writer. This appeared in "The Bombay Chronicle."

Raja Harishchandra premiered at the Coronation Cinema in Mumbai.

By the way...
I was influenced by Raja Ravi Varma's paintings of the Hindu gods. This was evident in the depiction of various gods and goddesses in my mythological films.

Musicians

MELODY MASTERS who touched our souls

A composer can turn a bunch of squiggles into music so powerful that it casts a spell on you. Meet a few such mesmerizing musicians.

A swaramandal is used as an accompanying instrument by Hindustani classical vocalists.

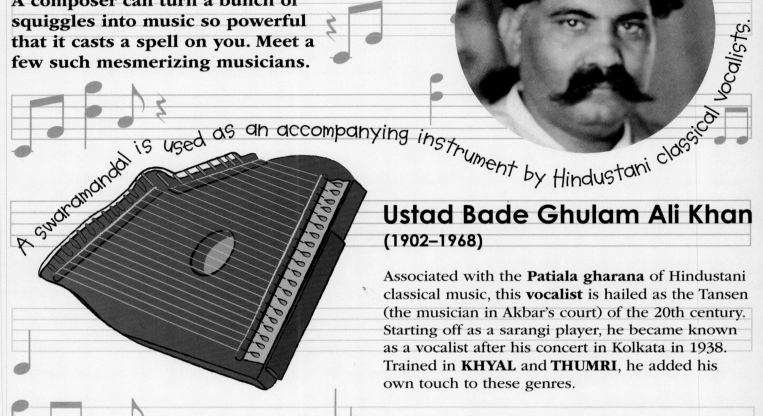

Ustad Bade Ghulam Ali Khan
(1902–1968)

Associated with the **Patiala gharana** of Hindustani classical music, this **vocalist** is hailed as the Tansen (the musician in Akbar's court) of the 20th century. Starting off as a sarangi player, he became known as a vocalist after his concert in Kolkata in 1938. Trained in **KHYAL** and **THUMRI**, he added his own touch to these genres.

Ustad Bismillah Khan
(1916–2006)

This musician from Varanasi took the **shehnai** from the confines of wedding halls to the world stage. He had the **rare honour of performing** at the Red Fort, New Delhi, on the eve of **INDEPENDENCE DAY** in 1947. He is only the third musician to be awarded the **Bharat Ratna** – India's highest civilian award.

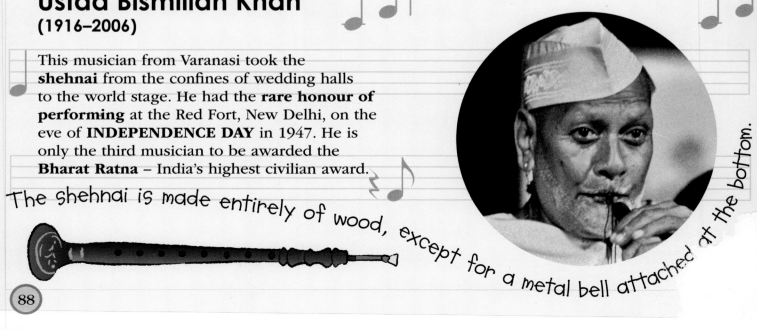

The shehnai is made entirely of wood, except for a metal bell attached at the bottom.

A 25-stringed instrument, the sarod has a deep resounding sound.

Ustad Ali Akbar Khan
(1922–2009)

Trained by his father, **Allauddin Khan**, the well-known musician of the Maihar gharana, this sarod player became a court musician for the **MAHARAJA OF JODHPUR**. Violinist Yehudi Menuhin, who took the maestro to the USA, hailed him as the *greatest musician* of the world.

Kishori Amonkar
(b. 1931)

A noted Hindustani classical vocalist, Kishori Amonkar trained under her mother, Mogubai Kurdikar of the **Jaipur gharana**. While following the finer points of the gharana, Amonkar frequently departed from the conventional style, adding features of other traditions. She has also sung for a few films, such as *Geet Gaya Patharon Ne* and *Drishti*.

The Jaipur gharana follows a khayal-based singing style.

The flute is a wind instrument, and is shaped like a tube.

Pandit Hariprasad Chaurasia
(b. 1938)

Unlike many other musicians who inherited the art from their parents, this flute player from Allahabad does not belong to any **music family**. As a teenager, he started learning vocal music, but a *chance hearing* of Pandit Bhola Ram's flute recital led him towards the wood instrument. Over time, Chaurasia has emerged as the foremost flute player of India.

Pandit Ravi Shankar

MAESTRO of the strings

Ravi Shankar was a sitar player, widely credited for making Indian classical music popular in the West.

By the way...
my two daughters, Anoushka Shankar and Norah Jones, are acclaimed musicians. Anoushka plays the sitar and Norah sings and plays the piano and guitar.

The Paris impact

Ravi Shankar (1920–2012) was born in a Bengali family in Varanasi. At the age of 10, he *moved to Paris with his brother*, choreographer Uday Shankar, and joined his dance troupe. While in Paris, young Ravi Shankar learned **Indian music and dance** as part of his brother's troupe, and also got a glimpse of **Western art and culture**. This unique combination of the East and West was to one day make him a **FORMIDABLE FORCE IN THE WORLD OF MUSIC**.

Young Shankar performing in his brother's dance troupe.

Shankar collaborated with Satyajit Ray on many occasions, starting with the Apu Trilogy.

The Indian stage

In 1938, Shankar moved back to India to *learn the sitar* from the renowned teacher Ustad Allauddin Khan. Later, he set out to **compose music for radio and films.** He recomposed the popular patriotic song **"SARE JAHAN SE ACCHA"**. He entered the world of cinema with Satyajit Ray's Apu Trilogy, the three films that trace the "coming of age" story of a young Bengali boy, for which Shankar composed the music.

He couldn't have done it without...

Famous music teacher and instrumentalist of the 20th century, **USTAD ALLAUDIN KHAN** *was the sitar guru of Ravi Shankar.*

East meets West

By the late 1950s, Ravi Shankar began performing for **international audiences** in the UK, USA, and Europe. His music influenced many musicians of that era, including *George Harrison* of the Beatles, who was so moved by Shankar's music that he **travelled to India to learn the sitar from him**. His association with Harrison became even more significant when the two decided to organize the **CONCERT FOR BANGLADESH** to raise funds for the victims of armed violence and ferocious flooding in Bangladesh. Held at the Madison Square Garden in the USA, in 1971, it featured performers such as **Bob Dylan, Eric Clapton, Shankar, and Harrison**.

The gift of music
Ravi Shankar is credited for building a large fan following for Indian music in the West. He won many awards and honours, including 14 honorary degrees and three Grammys. Back home, he was awarded the Padma Bhushan, the Padma Vibhushan, the Bharat Ratna, and the Ramon Magsaysay Award.

He paved the way for...

Ravi Shankar inspired George Harrison of the Beatles to compose SONGS WITH A DISTINCT INDIAN SOUND, *including* "ACROSS THE UNIVERSE" *and* "WITHIN YOU WITHOUT YOU".

The Concert for Bangladesh started the trend of CHARITY CONCERTS, *including the recently held Concert for Sandy Relief in USA.*

MS Subbulakshmi

The GODDESS of devotional songs, who held her bhaktas in thrall

All about me

- **BORN:** 1916
- **DIED:** 2004
- **PLACE OF BIRTH:** Madurai, Tamil Nadu
- **FACTOID:** I was the first Indian musician to be awarded the Ramon Magsaysay Award.
- **IN A NUTSHELL:** I was a leading exponent of Carnatic music, and my fans included Mahatma Gandhi and Pandit Nehru.

By the way...
I was able to reach a wider audience due to my ability to sing in more than 10 Indian regional languages.

A new shade of Kancheepuram sari called MS Blue is named after the singer.

An early start

Madurai Shanmukhavadivu Subbulakshmi was fondly called MS by her fans. MS was trained in Carnatic music by her mother and in Hindustani music by Pandit Narayan Rao Vyas. She released her first album at the *age of 10*, and gave her first public performance at the age of 13 at the **MADRAS MUSIC ACADEMY**. She particularly liked singing hymns by Mira, Tulsidas, Kabir, and Surdas.

Striking the right note

MS also dabbled in cinema, debuting in a Tamil film *Sevasadanam* in 1938. She played the lead role in the famous film *Bhakta Meera*. Her **devotional songs** in the film were instant hits. However, films didn't hold her interest for long, and she went back to her old **LOVE – MUSIC**. Her concerts at the Carnegie Hall, New York; UN General Assembly; and the Royal Albert Hall, London, brought her international recognition.

Ustad Zakir Hussain

The percussion artist who took the TABLA to the world stage

All about me

- **BORN:** 1951
- **PLACE OF BIRTH:** Mumbai, Maharashtra
- **FACTOID:** My father, the legendary tabla player Allah Rakha, introduced me to the percussion instrument when I was just two days old.
- **IN A NUTSHELL:** I love to collaborate with great musicians and experiment with different genres.

By the way... I won the first-ever Grammy Award for "Best World Music Album" for *Planet Drum*, in 1992.

The ultimate "ustad"

Zakir Hussain's first stage performance was at the age of six when he performed impromptu with the famous sarod player Ustad Akbar Ali Khan. His *spontaneity and stage presence* grabbed everybody's attention. A **child prodigy**, Hussain started touring the world with his father, Allah Rakha, at the **AGE OF 12**.

World musician

Zakir Hussain loves to improvise his compositions, experimenting with different genres of music. Known as the architect of the world music movement, the versatile musician founded the Indian fusion band *Shakti* with John McLaughlin, the British guitarist, and L Shankar, the famous violinist. He collaborated with George Harrison of **THE BEATLES** and other world musicians, such as Joe Henderson and Van Morrison. He even composed music for films such as *Heat and Dust*, *In Custody*, and *Little Buddha*.

John McLaughlin performed with Zakir Hussain at many concerts as part of the fusion band *Shakti*.

Satyajit Ray

India's first INTERNATIONALLY RECOGNIZED filmmaker

This filmmaker with a distinct style and approach showed the world that Indian cinema is not just Bollywood!

Did you know?
Satyajit Ray received an honorary Oscar for lifetime achievement in filmmaking in 1992.

Early life

Satyajit Ray (1921–1992) was born in Kolkata, West Bengal. His father, Sukumar Ray, was a prominent Bengali poet, and his grandfather, Upendrakishore Ray Chowdhury, was a distinguished writer as well. Ray had **exposure to books from a very early age**. His *love for films developed in school*, where he regularly read Hollywood trivia in magazines such as *Photoplay* and *Picturegoer*. He had a keen **interest in Western classical music** too.

Master storyteller

Ray chose the subjects of his films carefully, picking up stories by well-known writers, whether it was Bibhutibhushan Bandhyopadhyay (*Pather Panchali*, "Song of the Little World", 1955), Premchand (*Shatranj Ke Khiladi*, "Chess Players", 1977), or Tagore (*Ghaire Baire*, "Home and the World", 1984). These stories portrayed **human relationships and were told in a realistic way**. Besides social drama, Ray also made movies with themes from **FANTASY, SCIENCE FICTION, DETECTIVE STORIES, AND HISTORICAL DRAMA**. A complete filmmaker, he was involved with every aspect of cinema, including *writing scripts, composing the music, sketching the design, directing, and production.*

Sonar Kella ("Golden Fortress", 1974), written and directed by Ray, is a detective story about a six-year-old boy, Mukul, who gets kidnapped by some crooks.

He could not have done it without...

Ray studied at the Visva-Bharati University, founded by **RABINDRANATH TAGORE** (1861–1941). Here, Ray was exposed to various forms of art and culture.

UPENDRAKISHORE RAY CHOWDHURY (1863–1915), Ray's grandfather, was the founder of **SANDESH**, a Bengali magazine for children. Upendrakishore was also known for writing nonsense verses in the **TRADITION OF LEWIS CARROLL**

The magic world of Goopi-Bagha

Goopy Gyne Bagha Byne ("The Adventures of Goopi and Bagha", 1968), was Ray's adaptation of the **children's story written by his grandfather**. It is a **FANTASY FILM** where the two comic heroes, Goopy and Bagha, meet the *King of Ghosts* in the jungle, who *grants them three wishes* – to eat and travel on command and to play music that casts a spell. The film was later **followed by two sequels**.

Fascination with fiction

Ray created two hugely popular fictional characters in Bengali children's literature – Feluda, a detective, and Professor Shonku, a scientist. Feluda stories are narrated by his teenage cousin, Topshe. The science fiction of Shonku is presented as a diary discovered after the scientist mysteriously disappears.

Many people say that Feluda's character was modelled on Ray himself, as he shares Ray's love for trivia, his tall physique, and even a tendency to smoke heavily.

He paved the way for...

French filmmaker **JEAN RENOIR** (1894–1979) *was an inspiration to Ray, who followed his advice to show* REAL LIFE IN HIS FILMS, *avoiding the artificial melodrama of Hollywood cinema.*

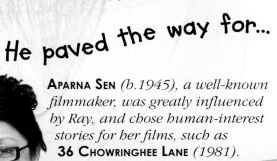

APARNA SEN (b.1945), a well-known filmmaker, was greatly influenced by Ray, and chose human-interest stories for her films, such as **36 CHOWRINGHEE LANE** (1981).

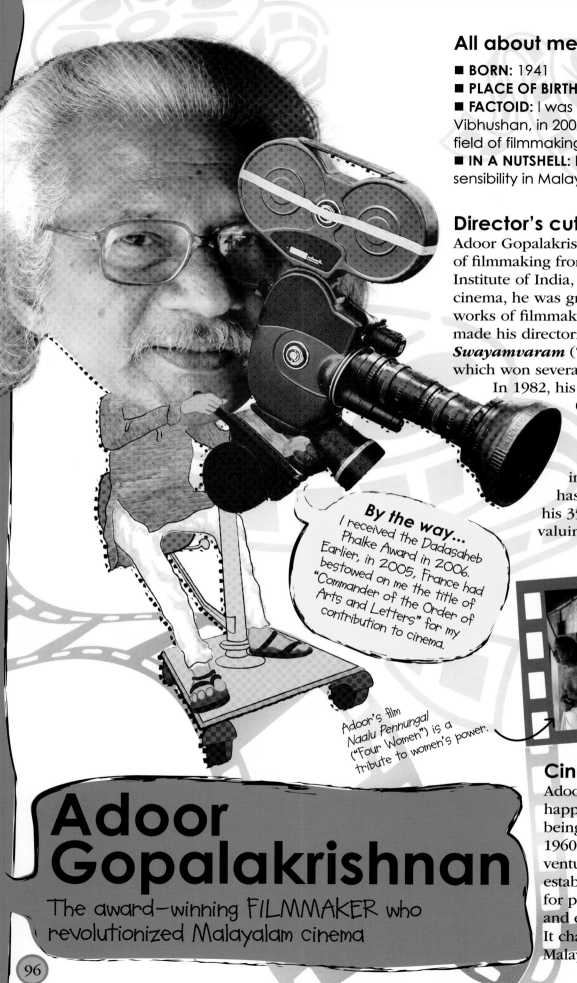

All about me

- **BORN:** 1941
- **PLACE OF BIRTH:** Adoor, Kerala
- **FACTOID:** I was awarded the Padma Vibhushan, in 2006, for my work in the field of filmmaking.
- **IN A NUTSHELL:** I ushered in a new sensibility in Malayalam cinema.

Director's cut

Adoor Gopalakrishnan learned the art of filmmaking from the Film and Television Institute of India, Pune. As a student of cinema, he was greatly inspired by the works of filmmaker Satyajit Ray. Adoor made his directorial debut in 1972 with **Swayamvaram** ("One's Own Choice"), which won several **national awards**.

In 1982, his film **Elippathayam** ("The Rat Trap") won the British Film Institute's award for the "most original and imaginative film". Adoor has made only 11 films in his 35-year-long career, clearly valuing quality over quantity.

By the way...

I received the Dadasaheb Phalke Award in 2006. Earlier, in 2005, France had bestowed on me the title of "Commander of the Order of Arts and Letters" for my contribution to cinema.

Adoor's film *Naalu Pennungal* ("Four Women") is a tribute to women's power.

Cinema revolutionary

Adoor Gopalakrishnan was not happy with the kind of films being made in Kerala in the 1960s. India's first co-operative venture, Chitralekha, was established by Adoor in 1965 for production, distribution, and exhibition of quality films. It changed the world of Malayalam cinema forever.

Adoor Gopalakrishnan

The award-winning FILMMAKER who revolutionized Malayalam cinema

All about me

- **BORN:** 1936
- **PLACE OF BIRTH:** Mumbai, Maharashtra
- **FACTOID:** There is a star with my name on the Hollywood Walk of Fame.
- **IN A NUTSHELL:** I have conducted the world's major orchestras, including the Los Angeles Philharmonic, New York Philharmonic, and Israel Philharmonic.

Zubin Mehta

The Indian MUSIC CONDUCTOR who conquered the world with his baton

Introduction to music

Zubin Mehta received his *first music lesson* from his father, Mehli Mehta, founder of the **BOMBAY SYMPHONY ORCHESTRA**. Mehta enrolled in pre-medical studies for a short while, but soon returned to his first love – music. He left for Vienna, Austria, in 1954, where he joined a **music conducting** programme. His music career got a head start when he won the Liverpool International Conducting Competition in 1958.

Zubin's orchestra at the Disney Concert Hall in Los Angeles, USA, in 2007.

By the way... the Israel Philharmonic Orchestra has conferred on me the title of "Music Director for Life".

All the world's a stage

Zubin Mehta has served as the music director of the Israel Philharmonic Orchestra, the Montreal Symphony Orchestra, and the Los Angeles Philharmonic, to name a few. Mehta **debuted as an opera conductor** with *Tosca*, a popular opera, in Montreal in 1963, going on to conduct in opera houses, such as the Metropolitan Opera, New York; the Vienna State Opera; and the *Royal Opera House, London*. Despite his fame, Mehta has not forgotten his roots in Mumbai, where he **runs a foundation** to train children in Western classical music.

Nek Chand

The artist who created gods out of WASTE

Nek Chand Saini is a self-taught artist who created beautiful sculptures with recycled junk.

Some of the waste material used by Nek Chand to make sculptures.

A life less ordinary

Nek Chand Saini (b. 1924) was **born in the village of Berian Kalan**, in present-day Pakistan. He came to Chandigarh in 1947 and joined the Public Works Department as a **road inspector in 1951.** This was when the Swiss architect Le Corbusier was redesigning the city, and razing the old Chandigarh down. Every day, after work, Nek Chand would collect **WASTE MATERIAL** from demolition sites and pile it in a nearby forest so that he could make use of the junk. He had to do this without the knowledge of the city authorities.

By the way...
While the state authorities did not support my project initially, they later heeded the public sentiment and allowed me to expand my secret garden, paying me a salary and 50 workers to fully devote myself to the Rock Garden.

He couldn't have done it without...

It took **MN Sharma** (b. 1923), the chief architect of Chandigarh in the 1970s, some time to persuade authorities, but his efforts paid off, for the Rock Garden got the **RECOGNITION IT DESERVED.**

The **Nek Chand Foundation** was started by conservator **Anton Tony Rajer** (1952–2011) in 1997 to create awareness about the Rock Garden.

Visitors at the Rock Garden, Chandigarh

The kingdom of gods
Nek Chand chose a secluded gorge in the forest, hidden from prying eyes, to create a **MAGIC KINGDOM**. He would disappear into the gorge at night and spend hours making sculptures out of waste. He had never stopped *missing his village* and found solace in recreating it on a small scale, complete with houses, shops, temples, rivers, and a carefully shaped landscape. **He saw human faces in the rocks** he collected, imagining them as "gods and goddesses" that inhabited his kingdom.

Treasure unearthed
Eighteen years after he created a huge treasure of sculptures, Nek Chand decided to share his vision with Chandigarh's **chief architect** of the time, **MN Sharma**. The architect was astounded to discover 12 acres of statues, courtyards, man-made waterfalls, and pathways that Chand had been patiently working on every night. Sharma advised Chand to continue his work in secret, until he convinced the authorities to acknowledge the masterpiece that later came to be known as the **ROCK GARDEN**. *In 1976*, the garden was finally opened to visitors.

A tourist paradise
An estimated 5,000 people from all over the world visit the Rock Garden every day. Situated near Sukhna Lake and spread across 40 acres of land in Chandigarh, the Rock Garden is India's second most popular tourist attraction, after the Taj Mahal.

Nek Chand sculpted human figures with broken bangles and cement.

He paved the way for...

MALAMPUZHA ROCK GARDEN, *Palakkad, Kerala, was the first such garden in south India. It was built in 1996 under* **NEK CHAND'S GUIDANCE.**

By cleverly using recycled junk and organic materials, **NEK CHAND INSPIRED** *a whole generation of* **RECYCLING ARTISTS** *to utilize waste material for their creations.*

Amrita Sher-Gil

The PAINTER who combined the best from the East and West

All about me
- **BORN:** 1913
- **DIED:** 1941
- **PLACE OF BIRTH:** Budapest, Hungary
- **FACTOID:** In 2006, my painting *Village Scene* sold for Rs 6.9 crore, the highest amount ever paid for a work of art in India.
- **IN A NUTSHELL:** I dominated the Indian art scene in the 1930s.

Life of an artist

Born to an Indian father and a Hungarian mother, Amrita Sher-Gil was one of the **MOST PROMINENT ARTISTS** of her time. Sher-Gil went to Paris in 1929, where she learned the basics of art at the *École des Beaux-Arts, the premier art school of the time*. In the mid-1930s, she returned to India with her family. Here, her painting style underwent a huge change, reflecting an Indian influence in the themes she chose. She also drew **inspiration from the cave paintings of Ajanta and Ellora**, in central India.

Bride's Toilet, captures Indian village life.

By the way...
I am the inspiration behind the popular Urdu play *Tumhari Amrita*, directed by Feroz Abbas Khan.

Work and recognition

Amrita died at the young age of 28, but left behind some great paintings that she is still remembered by. While her first major work, *Young Girls* (1932), shows the influence of European artists, her later paintings such as ***Bride's Toilet, South Indian Villagers Going to the Market,*** and *the Brahmacharis,* are distinctly Indian. Her paintings are **NATIONAL ART TREASURES** and adorn the galleries of the National Gallery of Modern Art, Delhi.

All about me

- **BORN:** 1915
- **DIED:** 2011
- **PLACE OF BIRTH:** Pandharpur, Maharashtra
- **FACTOID:** *Forbes* magazine once described me as the "Picasso of India".
- **IN A NUTSHELL:** Starting with cinema hoardings, I gradually made my way to become India's highest paid painter.

The magic brush

Maqbool Fida Husain **began as a painter of film posters** in Mumbai. In 1947, he was invited to join the Progressive Artists' Group by its founder and prominent painter, FN Souza. The same year, *his painting "Sunhera Sansaar" won an award* at an exhibition of the Bombay Art Society. This marked the beginning of a very successful career. Husain painted on many subjects, including **scenes from the *Ramayana* and *Mahabharata*** to iconic figures like Mahatma Gandhi and Mother Teresa.

MF Husain

The ARTIST who painted India on the world canvas

By the way...
a great admirer of Bollywood actor Madhuri Dixit, I dedicated a series of paintings to her.

Husain had a habit of walking without his shoes and would often travel barefoot.

Horses were a recurring theme in many of Hussain's paintings.

A man of many interests

Besides painting, Husain **MADE FILMS AS WELL**. His documentary, ***Through the Eyes of a Painter*** (1967), won the Golden Bear Award in the Berlin Film Festival. He directed several short films, as well as feature films like ***Gaja Gamini*** (2000), which starred Madhuri Dixit. Towards the end of his illustrious career, Husain was **forced to leave India** in 2006, when some sections of society objected to the way he portrayed Hindu deities in his paintings.

Amitabh Bachchan

The ANGRY YOUNG MAN of Bollywood

All about me

- **BORN:** 1942
- **PLACE OF BIRTH:** Allahabad, Uttar Pradesh
- **FACTOID:** I contested the Lok Sabha elections from Allahabad in 1984. I quit politics later, realizing it was not my cup of tea.
- **IN A NUTSHELL:** I ruled the Bollywood box office for more than four decades, delivering superhits such as *Deewar* (1975), *Namak Halal* (1982), *Agneepath* (1990), and *Black* (2005).

Rough road to the top

Amitabh Bachchan's journey to stardom was not an easy one. In the beginning, every filmmaker he approached thought he was *too tall or too dark to star in a film*. They did not approve of his deep voice either. Bachchan was **on the verge of giving up**, when *Saat Hindustani* (1969) came his way, fetching him the best newcomer award. This was followed by *several box-office flops* before he appeared in *Zanjeer* (1973) in a fiery role that earned him the title of the **ANGRY YOUNG MAN** of Bollywood.

By the way... in 2000, I began my television career as the host of the popular game show *Kaun Banega Crorepati*.

No looking back

His *popularity touched the sky* with the release of *Sholay* (1975), a film that became one of the **longest-running and most profitable** Indian movies ever. Ironically, it was the unique combination of his deep, baritone voice and dark, brooding looks that **set him apart from conventional heroes**, and made him an **ICON OF THE HINDI FILM INDUSTRY**.

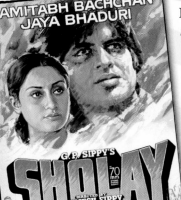

AMITABH BACHCHAN
JAYA BHADURI

G.P. SIPPY'S
SHOLAY
70 mm
DIRECTED BY RAMESH SIPPY

Sholay is the story of two petty thieves who help a policeman catch a ruthless bandit.

All about me

■ **BORN:** 1950
■ **PLACE OF BIRTH:** Bengaluru, Karnataka
■ **FACTOID:** I changed my name from Shivaji Rao Gaekwad to Rajinikanth at my director Balachander's suggestion.
■ **IN A NUTSHELL:** I worked as a bus conductor before becoming a movie star.

Rajinikanth

The SUPERSTAR known for his gravity-defying stunts

The first break

Shivaji Rao Gaekwad, popularly known as Rajinikanth, was enrolled at the Madras Film Institute to learn acting, when **K Balachander** – the legendary Tamil film director – selected him for the multi-starrer *Apoorva Raagangal* ("Rare Melodies") in 1975. The film required the Marathi-speaking actor to learn Tamil, a language he was not familiar with. Rajinikanth went on to rule Tamil cinema, launching his own brand of stylized acting and thrilling stunts – so loved by his fans.

Superstar or God?

Rajinikanth has acted in several blockbusters, such as *Sivaji*, in 2007, and *Enthiran* ("Robot"), in 2010, and has won many awards, including the **PADMA BHUSHAN,** for his contribution to cinema. However, it is not just the hits or the awards that have earned him a huge fan following. His admirers can't seem to have enough of his larger-than-life film persona or unique acting style. Some even consider him to be a god, bathing his posters in milk and praying for the success of his films.

By the way...
I am a household name in Japan, where all my films are regularly released. The Japanese version of the blockbuster *Enthiran* was released in 1,300 theatres across that country.

AR Rahman

The MOZART of Madras

All about me

- **BORN:** 1966
- **PLACE OF BIRTH:** Chennai, Tamil Nadu
- **FACTOID:** I changed my name from Dileep Kumar to " Alla Rakha Rahman" on the advice of an astrologer.
- **IN A NUTSHELL:** *Time* magazine has described me as the world's most prominent and prolific film composer.

Jingles to film music

Mani Ratnam, a popular Tamil film director, was looking for a music composer for his upcoming film *Roja*, (1992) when he heard some of **Allah Rakha Rahman's** advertising jingles. He liked the music and requested Rahman to score the music for his film. *The songs and the film were an instant success*, and brought in a lot of fame for the young music composer. There was no looking back for Rahman after this, and he went on to make many hit songs, such as **"Tuhi Re"** (*Bombay*, 1995) and **"Chaiyya Chaiyya"** (*Dil Se*, 1998).

> **By the way...**
> I composed a Punjabi song for the opening ceremony of the 2012 London Olympics.

Experiments with music

Rahman is known for experimenting with new sounds, creating a fusion of electronic, classical music, world music genres, such as reggae, and Indian folk sounds. His fame has now spread to foreign shores, with Hollywood directors queuing up to him to score music for their films. In 2008, his song "*Jai Ho*" for the English film *Slumdog Millionaire*, won him two Academy Awards and a Grammy.

All about me

- **BORN:** 1929
- **PLACE OF BIRTH:** Indore, Madhya Pradesh
- **FACTOID:** Popular singer Asha Bhonsle is my younger sister, and both of us were considered the unbeatable voices of Bollywood for a long time.
- **IN A NUTSHELL:** After a shaky start, I remained the queen of playback singing for more than five decades.

Lata loves diamonds and emeralds. In 2005, she designed a jewellery collection, Swaranjali.

By the way... apart from singing, I have composed music for some Marathi films, under the pseudonym Anand Ghan.

Initial struggles

Lata Mangeshkar's **music career started at the age of five**, when she assisted her father, a classical singer, in his musical plays. Unfortunately, her father passed away when she was only 13, and the responsibility of running the family fell on her shoulders. She tried her hand at acting in films but failed to make her mark. She then shifted her attention to playback singing but **HER THIN, HIGH-PITCHED VOICE DID NOT IMPRESS THE COMPOSERS** she met. After many rejections, Lata met eminent singer **Ghulam Haider, who thought she had potential**, and gave her a chance to sing in the 1948 film *Majboor – her first major break*.

She launched a perfume brand, Lata Eau de Parfume, in 2009.

Timeless voice

After her first break, **Lata rose to fame rapidly**. She worked with noted music directors and sang in many great films such as *Guide* (1965), *Amar Prem* (1972), and *Aandhi* (1975). Her *rendition of the patriotic song "Ae mere watan ke logo"*, remembering the martyrs of the Indo-China War in 1962, is said to have moved Pandit Jawaharlal Nehru, among many others, to tears.

Lata Mangeshkar

The MELODY queen of India

Sporting

Stars

"All work and no play makes Jack a dull boy."
These Indians took this adage too seriously and
made sports their full-time profession. Bringing
endless joy and excitement with each of their
wins, whether in chess, cricket, hockey, archery,
badminton, billiards, boxing, racing, or wrestling,
these sportspersons made sure there never was
a dull moment in our lives.

Dhyan Chand

The hockey WIZARD

All about me

- **BORN:** 1905
- **DIED:** 1979
- **PLACE OF BIRTH:** Allahabad, Uttar Pradesh
- **FACTOID:** The word "Chand" (moon) was added to my name as I mostly practised hockey at night.
- **IN A NUTSHELL:** I am the only Indian hockey player to win three Olympic golds.

In the Netherlands, the authorities broke Chand's hockey stick to check if there was a magnet inside.

From guns to hockey sticks

Dhyan Chand's tryst with hockey began after he **joined the army** at the age of 16. Prior to this, he had no interest in sports, although he loved wrestling. Thanks to a senior colleague who noticed Chand's dribbling skills in a few informal matches, he was encouraged to practise the sport. He made his international debut in 1926 in **New Zealand**, where he **helped India defeat** the host country. The win made him an instant **STAR OF HOCKEY**.

By the way... Hitler liked my technique so much that he offered me German citizenship and also the rank of colonel in his army.

Chand with the Indian hockey team during the Berlin Olympics, 1936

The Olympic hat-trick

Dhyan Chand's deft hockey moves won India **three successive Olympic medals**. The **first Olympic gold** came in 1928 in Amsterdam, where he was the top-scorer. Four years later, in the 1932 Olympics, he and his brother Roop Singh led India to victory, defeating Japan in the final match. His biggest moment came in 1936, when he captained the winning Indian team in the **BERLIN OLYMPICS**.

Milkha Singh

The FLYING SIKH who won several gold medals for India

The shoes that Milkha wore at the Rome Olympics in 1960 were later auctioned for Rs 24 lakh.

All about me

- **BORN:** 1929
- **PLACE OF BIRTH:** Lyallpur, Punjab (now in Pakistan)
- **FACTOID:** *Bhaag Milkha Bhaag* is a biographical film based on my life.
- **IN A NUTSHELL:** I was the first Indian athlete to win a gold medal at the Commonwealth Games.

Running for life

Milkha Singh was only 12 when he lost his parents during the 1947 partition riots. Forced to move to India from Pakistan, the young boy made a living by working at *roadside eateries*. He joined the Indian army, where he got to know that running in racing events could get him **an extra glass of milk**. To satisfy his appetite for milk, Singh started participating in athletic events. He tasted his first **SPORTING SUCCESS** in 1955 at the Services Athletic Meet, where he finished second in the 200m and 400m races.

Milkha often practised barefoot alongside a moving train to hone his athletic skills.

INDIA 171

By the way...
I declined the Arjuna Award in 2001, as I felt that it came 40 years too late.

A man of gold

Milkha Singh won 77 out of the 80 races he ran. He *struck gold* at the **Tokyo Asian Games** in 1958, winning both the 200m and 400m races. At the **COMMONWEALTH GAMES** held in Cardiff, Wales, the same year, he won a gold once again. His winning streak was broken when he narrowly missed the 400m bronze medal in the 1960 Rome Olympics. However, he redeemed his reputation when he beat Pakistani athlete Abdul Khaliq at the 1960 Indo-Pakistan meet in Lahore, earning him the title of the "Flying Sikh".

Tenzing Norgay

The Sherpa who conquered MOUNT EVEREST

All about me

- **BORN:** 1914
- **DIED:** 1986
- **PLACE OF BIRTH:** Khumbu, Nepal
- **FACTOID:** My parents named me Namgyal Wangdi but on the advice of a lama (a Buddhist priest) they changed it to Tenzing Norgay, which means luck.
- **IN A NUTSHELL:** Edmund Hillary and I were the first two men to reach Mount Everest's summit in 1953.

On reaching Everest's peak, Edmund Hillary took a picture of Tenzing posing with his ice-axe.

By the way... two teams were selected to climb Everest. While my team made it to the top, the other group was forced to turn back due to bad weather.

The brave Sherpa

Born in the **Sherpa community of Nepal**, Tenzing was drawn to mountaineering from an early age. He ran away to Darjeeling, India, to work as a **TREKKING PORTER**, and later took part in many *climbing expeditions*.

Tenzing ate a bar of mint cake on Everest and left behind a portion of it as a Buddhist offering.

On top of the world

At the age of 19, Tenzing was selected to join a **British expedition** to Mount Everest – at 8,848m (29,000ft), it is the highest mountain in the world. After many failed attempts to scale the mountain, the Sherpa – together with **EDMUND HILLARY** (1919–2008), a beekeeper and a mountaineering enthusiast from New Zealand – finally *succeeded in his mission* on **29 MAY 1953**. The two men enjoyed only 15 minutes at the summit because of thin air at the top.

All about me

- **BORN:** 1954
- **PLACE OF BIRTH:** Nakuri, Uttarakhand
- **FACTOID:** I left a small idol of goddess Durga on Mount Everest's peak and brought back some rock samples from the mountain.
- **IN A NUTSHELL:** I became the first Indian woman to climb Mount Everest, a record that can never be broken.

Bachendri Pal

The FIRST INDIAN WOMAN to reach the summit of Mount EVEREST

After reaching the peak, Pal stood there for nearly 43 minutes.

Never-say-die spirit

Bachendri Pal always dreamed of being a mountaineer, but not many people believed in her abilities. In 1982, during the course of a training, she climbed a pair of **glaciers: Gangotri at 6,675m (21,900ft) and Rudugaria 5,819m (19,091ft)**, proving her determination beyond any doubt. She was **SELECTED FOR INDIA'S FIRST MIXED TEAM**, (including both men and women) to climb Mount Everest. Early in the expedition, an avalanche buried the camp, leaving some team members injured. **Pal and the rest of her team refused to give up**, and finally reached the summit on 23 May 1984.

By the way...
in 2011, I inspired a housewife, Premlata Agarwal, to attempt to climb the Everest. At 48, she became the oldest Indian woman to have scaled the mountain.

Women power

Pal will always remain the first Indian woman to scale the Everest. But for her, an even bigger achievement was being able to **motivate and mentor other women** to take up mountaineering and other adventure sports. In 1993, she **LED AN ALL-WOMEN INDO-NEPALI TEAM** to Everest, which ended up creating seven world records. In 2007, she led the **Indian Women's First Thar Desert Expedition** (see above), a trek covering a distance of more than 2,000km (1,243 miles).

Prakash Padukone

The BADMINTON LEGEND who won nine singles titles

All about me

- **BORN:** 1955
- **PLACE OF BIRTH:** Bengaluru, Karnataka
- **FACTOID:** I was presented with the Arjuna Award in 1972 and the Padma Shri in 1982.
- **IN A NUTSHELL:** I won the National Senior title for nine years in a row, a record that has stayed unchallenged.

By the way... I was a defensive player, but after watching the legendary Indonesian badminton player Rudi Hartono, I adopted a more attacking style.

Starting early

Prakash Padukone was initiated into the game at an *early age* by his father, Ramesh Padukone, who was then the secretary of the Mysore Badminton Association. He started playing at the state junior level for Karnataka and **won the state junior championship title in 1964**, when he was only nine. Padukone made his mark at the **NATIONAL LEVEL** when he won the National Junior Badminton Championship in 1970.

Conquering the world

Prakash Padukone is one of the few Indian badminton players to find *success on foreign shores*. He won the gold medal in the men's singles event at the Canada Commonwealth Games in 1978. This was the beginning of a glorious chapter in his career during which he **won the Denmark Open and Swedish Open**, both in 1980. Later, in the same year, he won the **ALL ENGLAND OPEN BADMINTON CHAMPIONSHIP**, becoming the first Indian to achieve this feat.

All about me

- **BORN:** 1961
- **PLACE OF BIRTH:** New Delhi
- **FACTOID:** I was awarded the Arjuna Award in 1986, Padma Shri the same year, and the Rajiv Gandhi Khel Ratna in 1993.
- **IN A NUTSHELL:** I won eight world titles for billiards and one for snooker.

Geet Sethi

An eight–time world BILLIARDS champion

Born to play billiards

Geet Siriram Sethi started playing billiards at a young age. He took everyone by surprise when he defeated world champion Michael Ferreira, a fellow Indian, to win his first *National Billiards Championship* in 1982. He made a mark on the world stage when he won the **IBSF World Billiards Championship**, in 1985, against Australian billiards player Bob Marshall. Sethi created history by breaking the **WORLD RECORD** of 1,276 points in the 1992 World Professional Billiards Championship.

Chalk is applied to the tip of the cue stick, ideally before every shot, to increase the tip's friction.

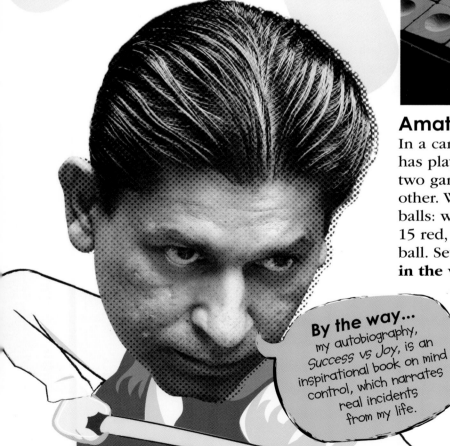

By the way... my autobiography, *Success vs Joy*, is an inspirational book on mind control, which narrates real incidents from my life.

Amateur snooker star

In a career spanning **30 YEARS**, Geet Sethi has played billiards as well as snooker. The two games are a little different from each other. While billiards is played with three balls: white, red, and yellow; snooker has 15 red, six of different colours, and one cue ball. Sethi became the **first amateur player in the world** to make the maximum break of 147 points in snooker, potting all the balls. In 2006, Sethi won a *world team snooker championship* in the USA. Although he hasn't formally announced his retirement from the game, Sethi hasn't played snooker since 2006.

Viswanathan Anand

The Indian CHESS GRANDMASTER

Viswanathan Anand is the only non-Russian to win the World Chess Championship five times.

The whiz kid

Viswanathan Anand (b. 1969) was born in Mayiladuthurai, Tamil Nadu, but spent most of his growing-up years in Chennai – **the chess capital of India**. He was *just six* when his mother began teaching him chess. Unlike other children of his age, Anand preferred chess shows to cartoons and chose **CHESS MAGAZINES** over comic strips.

Early wins

Success came early to Viswanathan Anand. It began in 1983 when Anand won the national sub-junior championship, at the young age of 14. The very next year, in 1984, he won the title of **International Master – the youngest Indian to achieve this feat**. Three years later, in 1987, when he won the world junior championship in the Philippines, he became the first Asian to do so. By 1988, he had turned India's **FIRST GRANDMASTER**.

He couldn't have done it without...

Viswanathan Anand's mother, **SUSHEELA ANAND** *(b. 1936), is his* **MENTOR** *who accompanied him to every tournament during the early phase of his career.*

Chess through the ages

Chess is believed to have originated in India around the 6th century CE. It is considered to be a refined version of a game called "*chaturanga*", often cited in the Indian epic *Mahabharata*. From India, the game spread to Persia (modern-day Iran) and then to Europe. Today, chess players test their skills against computers. In 1997, a man-made computer chess machine, "Deep Blue", defeated Garry Kasparov, then considered the best chess player of the world.

Terracotta chess pieces, excavated from the Indus Valley, bear a striking resemblance to modern chess pieces.

By the way...

in 2010, when volcanic ash eruptions from Iceland disrupted all flights, I drove from Spain to Bulgaria, a distance of 3,000km (1,865 miles), to play in the World Chess Championship. I defeated Bulgarian Veselin Topalov to win the title.

World champion

Viswanathan Anand had to wait till the year 2000 to win his **first World Chess Championship** title, when he beat Spain's Alexei Shirov (b. 1972) in the final. He ***reclaimed the title*** in 2007 and continued to hold it for the next three years. In 2012, he won the title **FOR THE RECORD FIFTH TIME**. This time he defeated Israel's Boris Gelfand (b. 1968) in a nerve-wracking tie-breaker.

American chess grandmaster and the 11th World Chess Champion **BOBBY FISCHER** *(1943–2008) made a* **HUGE IMPRESSION ON ANAND,** *who considers Fischer the greatest chess player of all time.*

Viswanathan Anand's wife, **ARUNA ANAND** *(b. 1974), doubles up as his* **MANAGER** *and schedules his interviews and travels.*

Sachin Tendulkar

This iconic batsman is the only cricketer to score 100 international centuries, and also the only one to make 30,000 runs in international cricket.

The GOD of cricket

Early life

Sachin Tendulkar (b. 1973) was born in Mumbai. The youngest of his siblings, Sachin was named after his family's favourite musician, **Sachin Dev Burman**. As a young boy, Sachin did not show much interest in academics, but was greatly attracted to athletics. His brother, Ajit, decided to tap his talent and took him to *Ramakant Achrekar, a top cricket coach*. Sachin proved his mettle at the age of 14 when he scored 329 runs in a school match.

The first of a hundred

Sachin was only 16 when he made his international debut in a Test match against Pakistan, in 1989 – he came back from the series with two half-centuries. However, he had to wait for another year to score his **first hundred, while playing against England**, in 1990 – he was 17 years, 82 days old then. By the time he turned 23, he was named *India's captain* for the 1996 **WORLD CUP**. Although he did not bring home the cup, he finished the tournament as the top scorer.

Sachin with Kapil Dev, the legendary bowler, and Azharuddin, an ace batsman, during his debut match.

He couldn't have done it without...

Sachin's brother, **AJIT RAMESH TENDULKAR**, *played a crucial role in shaping his career. He has also been Sachin's manager, planning his schedules and appointments.*

Super scorecard

Sachin Tendulkar retired from the world of cricket in 2012, but not before he had registered almost all records in his name. He became the first batsman to score a double century in One Day Inetrnational (ODI) cricket, in 2010, and also the only player to *record 100 international centuries*. Sachin has the rare feat of being the first batsman in history to get more than 15,000 runs in both Tests and ODIs. The master-blaster was also the **FIRST BATSMAN** to reach the 10,000-run milestone.

Sachin was part of the Mumbai Indians 2011 Champions League Twenty20 winning team.

By the way...
as a kid, I was a huge fan of tennis player John McEnroe. I grew my hair long to look like him and made my father buy me the same headbands McEnroe wore.

Sudhir Kumar Chaudhary is usually seen in tricolour body art, waving the national flag in all the matches played by India.

Recognition follows

Sachin Tendulkar's records can be only matched by the recognition he has received from all corners of the world. He is the first sportsperson and youngest Indian to be awarded the **Bharat Ratna** at the age of 40. *Sir Don Bradman*, the Australian legend, included him in his "dream team". The master-blaster is also the first Indian sports personality whose wax statue stands at Madame Tussauds, London.

Crazy fan

Sachin's consistent performances earned him a fan following like no other sportsperson. People know Sudhir Kumar Chaudhary as Sachin's most ardent fan. He is usually seen in tricolour body art, waving the national flag in all the matches played by India across the globe. He has also had the distinction of lifting the 2011 World Cup trophy along with Tendulkar.

Dronacharya Awardee **RAMAKANT ACHREKAR** *was Sachin's* **FIRST COACH** *who trained him to become a world-class batsman.*

SUNIL GAVASKAR, *the batsman who made a record 34 Test centuries,* **INSPIRED SACHIN** *to match his feat. He even gifted Sachin a pair of his leg guards.*

Mary Kom

The boxer who PUNCHED her way to success

Mary Kom overcame her tough life in Manipur to become a five-time boxing champion.

Early life

Mary Kom (b. 1983) was born in a poor tribal family in Manipur. Her grandmother named her **Chungneijang**, which means "*prosperous*" in the Kom tribe's dialect. As a schoolgirl, Mary enjoyed participating in different athletic events, and hoped that sports would one day **BAIL HER FAMILY OUT OF POVERTY**.

Did you know?
Sanjay Leela Bhansali, the famous Bollywood director, has planned a film on Mary Kom's life. The film will be released in October 2014.

DHISHUM

DHISHUM!

↑
Punching bags are filled with grains, sand, rags, or other material, and are usually hung from the ceiling or fixed to a stand.

Hands in glove

In 1998, Dingko Singh, a boxer from Manipur, **won a gold medal** at the Asian Games, motivating many young boys and girls, including Mary, to get into the boxing ring. Mary moved to Imphal to train under the boxing coach **Ibomcha Singh** and *in 2001 won a silver medal* in the **WORLD BOXING CHAMPIONSHIP** in the USA. The next year, she won the gold in Turkey.

Magnificent Mary

The government of India has acknowledged Mary's many successes by awarding her the Padma Bhushan, Arjuna Award, and Rajiv Gandhi Khel Ratna award. In 2009, she was made the ambassador of women's boxing for the International Boxing Association. She also features on the list of "25 most influential women" brought out by the Limca Book of Records.

By the way...
I wrote my autobiography *Unbreakable* to inspire readers to have passion, dedication, and faith in themselves.

The supermom

In 2006, Mary gave birth to twins, and took a break from boxing to raise her newborns. After two years of absence, she entered the ring again in 2008 during the **WORLD CHAMPIONSHIP** at Ningbo, China. The mother of two *surprised everyone with a gold medal*. She has won **twelve gold, two silvers, and two bronze medals**, including the one at the 2012 London Olympics until now.

The boxer with her children, Rengpa and Naimai, at her residence.

She couldn't have done it without...

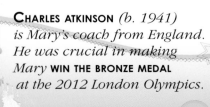

IBOMCHA SINGH (b. 1960) *is a Dronacharya award-winning boxing coach. He was the* **FIRST COACH** *to train Mary.*

CHARLES ATKINSON (b. 1941) *is Mary's coach from England. He was crucial in making Mary* **WIN THE BRONZE MEDAL** *at the 2012 London Olympics.*

Champions league

SPORTING heroes that made India proud

For these men and women, sports is not just fun and games. Years of hard work and discipline helped them achieve sporting success and win medals for India.

PT Usha
(b. 1964)

Thekkeparambil Usha was born in Payyoli, Kerala, Pilavullakandi, and is fondly called the **"PAYYOLI EXPRESS"** in recognition of her many sprinting successes. She first shot into limelight when she won **two silver medals** at the **Delhi Asian Games in 1982**. Her haul of four gold medals and a silver at the Seoul Asian Games in 1986 won her the title "Golden Girl". In all, she has won **102 medals** in various national and international athletic meets.

"queen of Indian track and field".

PT Usha is often called the

Abhinav Bindra
(b. 1982)

Abhinav was so determined to win an Olympic medal that he got an *indoor shooting range* built in his house. This marksman's dedication and never-say-die attitude helped him to look past his defeat at the 2004 Athens Olympics and win the **GOLD MEDAL AT THE 2008 BEIJING OLYMPICS**. He became the first Indian to win an individual gold medal at the Olympics.

Sushil Kumar Solanki
(b. 1983)

This wrestling champion from Haryana grew up on a diet of ghee, milk, and green vegetables. Poor training facilities did not deter Sushil from pursuing his Olympic dream. He won a bronze medal in **66kg FREESTYLE WRESTLING** at the 2008 Beijing Olympics, and a silver medal at the 2012 London Olympics, becoming the **first Indian** to win *consecutive individual Olympic medals*.

Saina Nehwal
(b. 1990)

This young badminton player has many "firsts" to her name. From being the first Indian to win the **World Junior Badminton Championship** in 2008 to becoming the first Indian to win three Super Series titles in Indonesia and Singapore between 2009 and 2011, Saina has been there and done that. When she won a bronze medal in badminton at the **2012 LONDON OLYMPICS**, she became the only Indian to have done so, yet again.

World champions

Deepika Kumari
(b. 1994)

At the age of 12, this daughter of an auto-rickshaw driver became the **Junior World Archery Champion**, when she won the compound individual gold medal in 2006. A string of outstanding performances on the home turf conditioned Deepika to win an individual and a team **GOLD MEDAL** at the 2010 Commonwealth Games. She went on to win the **2012 World Cup in Turkey** and became the **WORLD NUMBER ONE** in women's archery at the age of 18, proving once again that age is just a number.

Let's applaud...

They may not have made the top 100 – but these TOP PEOPLE made a top contribution to INDIAN HISTORY

Valmiki (1st millennium BCE)

Once a highway dacoit, Valmiki later mended his ways and became a sage. He wrote the famous Sanskrit epic, the *Ramayana*, which tells the story of Rama – a virtuous king.

Prithviraj Chauhan (1149–1192)

This fearless Rajput warrior-king fought many battles to extend and protect his kingdoms of Ajmer and Delhi. He pitted his strength against Muslim invader Muhammad Ghori and managed to kick him out of Delhi.

Historically, the sword evolved from the dagger around 3000BCE.

Razia Sultana (1205–1240)

The first woman ruler of India, Razia Sultana led her army riding on an elephant. She was not only brave but a wise, efficient ruler. To fit into the male-dominated world, she only wore men's clothes.

Mirza Ghalib (1797–1869)

From the Mughal era to this day, the poems of Urdu and Persian poet Mirza Ghalib have touched hearts and minds. Many of his poems are set to music in the popular lyric form known as ghazal.

Dadabhai Naoroji (1825–1917)

A social and political leader for almost 60 years, Dadabhai Naoroji was known as the "Grand Old Man" of India. He was one of the founders of the Indian National Congress, the nationalist party formed in 1885.

Bal Gangadhar Tilak (1856–1920)

A fiery leader of the Indian freedom struggle, Tilak gave the slogan "Swaraj (self-rule) is my birthright, and I shall have it!" He spearheaded the Swadeshi Movement to boycott foreign goods and was sent to jail many times.

C Rajagopalachari (1878–1972)

The first (and only) Indian Governor-General of India after independence, C Rajagopalachari was an eminent statesman, scholar, and thinker. Jawaharlal Nehru said that he "represents the highest type of mind in India".

GD Birla (1894–1983)

The Birla chain of business is a vital part of Indian industry and the man who established the vast network of sugar, paper, and other goods was GD Birla. He was a close associate of Mahatma Gandhi.

Vinoba Bhave (1895–1982)

Called the acharya, or "teacher", Vinoba Bhave led the Bhoodan Movement in which he asked people to donate land to the poor.

Kamaladevi Chattopadhyay (1903–1988)

Known as a rebel, this freedom fighter was a champion of women's rights and Indian art. She set up the All India Handicrafts Board to revive crafts like toymaking, weaving, and pottery, and brought them to international attention.

Chandrashekhar Azad (1906–1931)

This fiery freedom fighter tried to blow up a train in 1926 and shot a British police officer in 1928. He wanted complete independence from the British and died fighting for it.

RK Narayan (1906–2001)

A prolific novelist, RK Narayan was one of the first Indians who wrote in English to win international acclaim. His first novel *Swami and Friends* (1935) was followed by 34 more, mostly centred on the fictional town of Malgudi peopled with memorable characters.

Bhagat Singh (1907–1931)

A revolutionary in the Indian fight for freedom, Shaheed Bhagat Singh believed in action. He threw two bombs in a government assembly hall to protest against the British. He was later hanged for this and became a martyr (Shaheed).

Sam Maneckshaw (1914–2008)

The Indian army's first Field Marshal and the eighth Army Chief, Sam Maneckshaw served the Indian army for over 40 years. In 1971, he led the Indian forces to victory in the war against Pakistan.

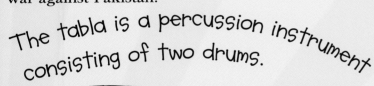

The tabla is a percussion instrument consisting of two drums.

Alla Rakha (1919–2000)

Rhythm was tabla maestro Alla Rakha's forte, his wizardry in knocking out beats electric. He accompanied many soloist players, but he most often travelled with sitarist Ravi Shankar, delighting audiences all over the world.

Satish Dhawan (1920–2002)

As head of the Indian space programme and chairman of the Indian Space Research Organization (ISRO), this rocket scientist propelled India into the big league of space-faring nations in the use of satellites, telecommunications, and remote sensing.

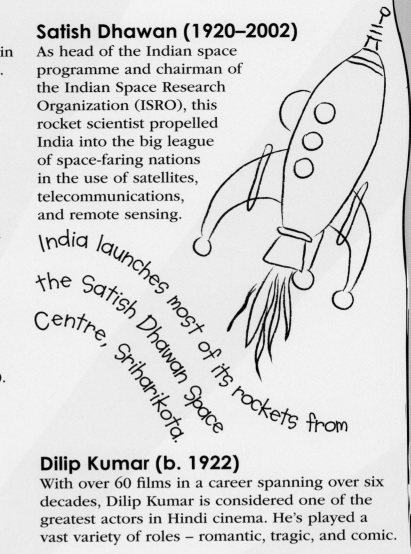

India launches most of its rockets from the Satish Dhawan Space Centre, Sriharikota.

Dilip Kumar (b. 1922)

With over 60 films in a career spanning over six decades, Dilip Kumar is considered one of the greatest actors in Hindi cinema. He's played a vast variety of roles – romantic, tragic, and comic.

Atal Bihari Vajpayee (b. 1924)

Poet and orator, Vajpayee was the 11th Prime Minister of India (13 days in 1996 and again in 1998–2004). A leader of the Bharatiya Janata Party, he was the only non-Congress party Prime Minister to serve the full five-year term.

RK Laxman (b. 1924)

India's best-loved cartoonist, RK Laxman created the Common Man, the cartoon character that delighted Indians since 1951. Featured in the cartoon strip "You Said It" in *The Times of India*, it captured the daily lives of common Indians.

APJ Kalam (b. 1931)

He was the 11th President of India (2002–2007), but that's not Kalam's only feat. This aeronautical engineer helped develop India's first Satellite Launch Vehicle (SLV-III) and other space missiles, making India part of the international space club.

Dhirubhai Ambani (1932–2002)

The son of a school teacher, business tycoon Dhirubhai Ambani built Reliance Industries, an empire of textile manufactures, petroleum products, telecommunications, and financial services, from scratch and became the owner of India's largest oil refinery.

Madhubala (1933–1969)

In the 1950s, Madhubala was the reigning star of Bollywood. A leading American magazine called her the "Biggest Star in the World". Among her 70 films, *Mughal-e-Azam* (1960) is still ranked as the second-biggest Bollywood box office hit.

CNR Rao (b. 1934)

A giant figure in the field of chemistry, Dr Rao was conferred the Bharat Ratna in 2013. He has written 45 books and 1,500 research papers over five decades. He also headed the Scientific Advisory Council to the Prime Minister of India.

Rao's main work has been in the field of solid-state chemistry.

Salman Rushdie (b. 1947)

Salman Rushdie is a well-known novelist in the English language. His second novel, *Midnight's Children*, won the prestigious Booker Prize in 1981. *The Times* has listed him among the "50 greatest writers since 1945".

Sunil Gavaskar (b. 1949)

An outstanding opening batsman, Sunil Gavaskar captained the Indian team in the 1970s and 80s. For two decades, he held the record of scoring 34 Test centuries.

Azmi has appeared in over 120 films in both mainstream and independent cinema.

Shabana Azmi (b. 1950)

One of the finest Indian actresses, Shabana Azmi is acclaimed for her real-life character portrayals in Indian films that are different from the typical romances of Bollywood.

Anish Kapoor (b. 1954)

Renowned for his public sculptures and installation art, Anish Kapoor uses materials ranging from marble to stainless steel and red wax. His works include *Cloud Gate* in the Millennium Park, Chicago, and *ArcelorMittal Orbit* in London's Olympic Park.

Kapil Dev (b. 1955)

One of the greatest all-rounders in the game of cricket, Kapil Dev was the captain of the Indian cricket team that won the 1983 Cricket World Cup. A pace bowler, he took more than 400 wickets in Test matches.

Indra Nooyi (b. 1955)

From 2008 onwards, Indra Nooyi has been listed as one of the world's 100 most powerful women by *Forbes* magazine. She is currently the chairperson and CEO of PepsiCo, the world's second-largest food and beverage business.

Leander Paes (b. 1973)

With his never-say-die attitude, this tennis player has won eight doubles and six mixed doubles Grand Slam titles, among many others. He won a bronze medal in the 1996 Atlanta Olympic Games.

Leander Paes shot to international fame when he won the 1990 Wimbledon Junior title.